THE NATIC

i.

THE PUBLIC SECTOR BORROWING REQUIREMENT

AN INTERIM BALANCE SHEET

Also by Stanley Trevor

Poetry

World In Action, (Hippopotamus Press). Chaka's Rock, (Anarcho Press). Reflections (As in Water) – A Partita & Fugue, (Tapocketa Press). Elegiacs for Jean. (Anarcho Press), Guerrilla.(Writer's Forum), Hard Bones – Some poems for Voices, (Writer's Forum), Lollipops – A Book of Light(ish) Verse, (Anarcho Press), Continuum, (Writer's Forum), La Creation Du Monde – A Libretto designed to be performed in conjunction with Darius Milhaud's composition of that name, 1922, (Anarcho Press).

Prose

The Marriage of Heaven & Hell – A Celebration (Anarcho Press), On the Concrete Poetry of Bob Cobbing – A Tribute (Anarcho Press).

STANLEY TREVOR

THE NATIONAL DEBT

i.e.

THE PUBLIC SECTOR BORROWING REQUIREMENT

AN INTERIM BALANCE SHEET

Illustrated by
PHIL EVANS

contributors include
HEINRICH HEINE
WILLIAM COBBETT

Anarcho Press

distributed by
AK Distributors

First Published – June 1994

Anarcho Press
30 Greenhill
Hampstead High Street
London NW3 5UA

Distributed by:
AK Distributors
22 Lutton Place
Edinburgh EH8 9PE

ISBN No. 0 906469 18 X

Acknowledgements (with many
thanks for assistance):

Labour Party Research Library

Greenpeace

Campaign for Nuclear Disarmament

Campaign against the Arms Trade

Low Pay Unit

Ken Livingstone's Office,
House of Commons.

Cover Image: Phil Evans

ABOUT THE AUTHOR

Stanley Trevor was amongst the first wave of immigrants from South Africa after World War 2.

During the fifties and sixties he wrote for and collaborated in the production of the magazine 'Contemporary Issues', being the collective organiser for a radical international (Anglo–American–German–South African) democratic movement. Later, in the sixties and early seventies, he edited the magazine 'Confrontation', for which he wrote on various subjects. This magazine was innovative and influential in the 'student movement' and the so–called 'new left'.

In the mid–seventies, he retired from political work to pursue career as an architect and to write poetry.

He was the only white poet (one of fifteen readers) to be invited to read at a memorial reading at the Kiskidee Centre in Islington for Steve Biko and Robert Sobukwe, a signal honour.

He was also active during the seventies in the Poetry Society and now holds the position of coordinator of the Association of Little Presses.

"....while one places in front of all institutions the name of the King, as 'the King's Army',' the King's Navy',' the King's courts', 'the King's Prisons' etc., yet, notwith-standing, the great debt, which really owes its origins to those institutions, is never called the King's debt; and it is the only institution by which the nation is shown the honour of having something named after her!" *William Cobbett.*

THE DEBT

Treasury Forecast[1]*   £50,000,000,000

CONSTITUENTS OF THE DEBT

A RANDOM SAMPLING
(which could be increased a hundred fold)**

Privatisation**	£43,125,600,000
Black Wednesday – 16/9/1992	17,000,000,000[2]
Poll Tax	3,500,000,000[3]
Trident Missile Programme**	33,000,000,000[4]
Headquarters for MI5/MI6 etc.	1,500,000,000[5]
Nuclear Levy**	9,100,000,000
Thorp Reprocessing Plant**	2,800,000,000
Tax Reduction	14,000,000,000[6]
Tax Evasion**	2,000,000,000
Gulf War	2,464,000,000[7]
British Army of the Rhine	1,275,440,000[8]
The War in Ireland	1,000,000,000[9]

Interest on all of the above
etc. etc. etc.

* For numbered notes, see Appendix.
** See Glossary of Technical Terms

1

GLOSSARY OF TECHNICAL TERMS

Privatisation:
Late 20th century equivalent of the enclosures; a present from the privateers of England to the privateers of England; the illegal expropriation of public property and its sale through the mechanism of the stock market to receivers of stolen goods.

COST

Underpricing of shares:	£ 4,000,000,000[1]
Dividends (1984 – 1991)	4,146,000,000
Undervaluation (electricity):	16,900,000,000[2]

---

1. All figures, unless otherwise stated, quoted from Document 2.4A, being a summary of 'Labour's Privatisation Dossier' dated September 1991, printed and published by the Labour Party.

2. This represents the gap between auditor's valuations of electricity industry assets and proceeds received by the tax–payer. The figure has been quoted for *electricity only* as a case study. Similar figures could be obtained for all industries privatised. It is worth noting that when those industries were 'nationalised' or 'brought under public control' they were in fact *bought* under public control. The most notorious feature of nationalisation was that the sections in the economy chosen for nationalisation were characterised by technical obsolescence, under–capitalisation, and were unprofitable, requiring reorganisation, re–equipping, and recapitalisation at a cost which private enterprise was neither able nor ready to meet. 'Nationalisation' was the means whereby the British taxpayer was coerced into providing direct financial relief for the private sector in respect of bankrupt industries on top of

Debt write–offs	17,679,600,000
Fees/Commissions/Advice	1,400.000,000
"Green Dowry" (Water)	1,000,000,000
	£43,125,600,000

Market:

An artificial socially created structure controlling distribution of commodities through the mediation of money designed to enable the products of labour to be purchased cheap and sold dear, thus ensuring the continuing enrichment of the rich and impoverishment of the poor.

Note: Profit motive unknown in Nature which revolves entirely around subsistence!

Market Forces:

The detailed mechanisms of the parasitism as realised through the market.

In a television interview, President Nyerere of Tanzania asked the following question:–

---

which the old owners were "compensated" – e.g. the alarming deficit of £25,000,000 in the accounts of the coal mining industry (1947) included significantly the figure of £13,000,000 due to the old owners, who, one might say, by not ploughing profits back into the various industries as reinvestment, had already overcompensated themselves in the form of dividends. This was called 'socialism!'

"Last year, when we exported a ton of sisal to Britain, we could purchase certain goods with the money we received. This year, in order to purchase the same amount of goods, we have to sell two tons of sisal. What I want to know is – what happened to that other ton of sisal?"

Answer: "That was just bad luck due to the fall of prices for primary products on the world market."

"Well then, the nations of the world must learn to share the bad luck! But this does not answer my question. What I want to know is – what happened to that other ton of sisal?"

Real answer: It disappeared into the fat maw of the West.

This is known as:–

GATT:

General Agreement on Tariffs and Trade – Sanctions applied to the Third World (euphemistically referred to as the 'Developing Nations') to ensure control of the world market.

A columnist reporting on the Gatt talks in the Observer stated: (12/12/1993):–

> "But much of the developing [!] world – *regularly sidelined throughout the marathon talks* – [my

emphasis. S.T.] continues to question the equity of these rules."

By reducing tariffs in the primary producing countries, their markets will be flooded with cheap industrial products from the North and for the benefit of the North, but no investment capital reserves can be built up since the existing agreements negotiated before the GATT agreement which protected such products as, for example, cocoa and coffee from Kenya, have been done away with. The president of the African Development Bank stated on television that he could see no advantage for the African bean farmers. (BBC News, 14/11/1993).

Hot on this we learn that:–

"There will, of course [!] be winners and losers. Europe will gain £145 billion in world trade, but Africa will *lose* [my emphasis. S.T.] some £2.8 billion due to rises in the price of food resulting from the removal of subsidies! In addition, antidumping rules will militate against the penetration of the market by third world countries. (BBC News 15/11/1993).

According to a letter in the Guardian (3/11/1993):

"...the Gatt saga is less a Hollywood epic than an Australian soap. But its final episode, given a dramatic twist by the North American Free Trade Agreement (Nafta) sub plot, has profound implications for the future of the world's poorest countries and people.

"Reduced to their essentials, the Uruguay Round and Nafta offer a similar vision for the future – a world of free trade and deregulated markets. These, we are assured, will generate increased global investment, employment and income. The alternative, we are relentlessly told by commentators, is the doomsday prospect of 1930s–style trade wars and the collapse of the liberal trading order administered under Gatt auspices.

"Viewed from the South, the Trade war has already started. As the Uruguay Round has dragged on, the US preference for unilaterally bludgeoning open foreign markets to reduce its trade deficit has increased. Developing [!] countries protecting their financial service industries or refusing to accept US patent laws have been among the most prominent targets of trade sanctions [backed by the resources of the most powerful, ruthless, brutal, aggressive and destructive military capability the world has ever known – cf. Panama, the Gulf War, Somalia, etc., etc., as well as (more or less indirectly) the barbarism unleashed in South America – Salvador, Nicaragua, etc. S.T.] – not least because of their limited retaliatory capacity.

"Far from outlawing such practices, the new trade body which will emerge from the Uruguay Round, the Multilateral Trade Organisation, will institutionalise a system of cross–retaliation – a euphemism for allowing industrial countries to impose sanctions on the exports of developing [!] countries which fail to open up their markets. In other words, more of the same.

"This perversion [no! – *essential nature!* S.T.] of multi–

lateralism tells us much about the power of the trans-national corporations which have written large parts of the GATT script. For example, the new GATT regulations on the deregulation of financial services reflect the massive influence of American, European, and Japanese financial conglomerates seeking to improve their access to Third World markets. The upshot is that Third World governments will exercise less control over foreign investment [read 'no control whatsoever' – esp. in terms of their enormous *debt*, (PSBR, perhaps!) the payments of the interest on which alone are crippling! S.T.]."

According to a further report in the Guardian (10/1/1994):

"Repeated rounds of rescheduling have left Africa with a debt to export ratio of *400 per cent* [my emphasis. S.T.] higher than for Latin America at the peak of its debt crisis. Servicing Africa's debt currently drains the region of *more than a quarter* [my emphasis. S.T.] of its export earnings, or some £107 billion."

A winged word has it that poverty is the mother of tyranny. Can anyone doubt that the slaughter in Rawanda (for which non-payment of the army provided the spark) is the elemental result of the appalling poverty in the country where there is a shortage of everything (except, apparently, armaments, and where could they have come from?) has its ground in the appalling poverty of its people, this itself the direct result of Metropolitan policy as enshrined in GATT.

Nevertheless (there is no sentiment in business) The

World Development Movement reports:

> "British Banks will receive, in the end, seven billion dollars ($\pm$ £4 billion) in tax relief on provisions for Third World Debt." [3]

Another gift from the privateers....etc. Small wonder Sir Jeremy Morse, Chairman, Lloyds Bank lets it be known:

> "We have not written off our Third World Debt. We have provided for it, and that is a very important distinction."[4]

Yet another PSBR! The letter of 3/11/1993 continues:

> "Similarly, the new intellectual property regime will massively increase the costs of technology imports into 'developing' [!] countries, imposing what amounts to a US style patenting system. The upshot: massive profits for US companies and further marginalisation for the South. Meanwhile, Northern agro-chemical companies will be left free to exploit, without any payment, the seeds and other genetic materials developed over centuries by Third World communities. This obvious iniquity has provoked mass demonstrations in India, where rural communities rightly fear loss of control over their environment and food security.

---

4. Quoted by 'The World Development Movement' in their pamphlet 'Piggy Banks'.

4. Ibid

8

"And what about the losers from market liberalisation? In Mexico, small holder maize producers, the majority of whom farm plots in ecologically fragile (!) areas, face the prospect of a Nafta "free trade" deal which will expose them to competition from imports of American maize. Good for US grain companies, no doubt, but a disaster for the estimated two million Mexican farmers who will lose their livelihoods as a result."

Virtually predictably comes the news of the Zapatista peasant revolt in Southern Mexico. According to a report in the Guardian (4/1/1994):

"The rebels, most of them descendants of Maya, say cattle ranchers, in league with political barons, known as *caciques,* have robbed them of their land. "We possess nothing, absolutely nothing – no home, no land, no work, no education," their leaders said in a communique.

"The North American Trade Agreement, which binds Mexico's economy to the United States and Canada, would mean "the death of the indigenous peoples." Peasants growing maize on poor hillside land could not hope to compete with grain from the prairies [my emphasis S.T.]."

The letter of the 13/11/1993 continues:

"The ultimate failure [read: *"success"*: S.T.] of the Gatt and of Nafta is that, behind the free market smoke screen, *they place the strategic interests of powerful governments and corporations above the social and*

9

economic rights of vulnerable communities and poor countries. [my emphasis S.T.]"

Free Market:

An ideological invention designed to deceive the people into believing in the existence of free and universal competition.

a) According to Naom Chomsky, 45% of the world's trading is carried out between 10 major multi-national companies on a cartelized basis, i.e. agreed price fixing between producers and the withholding of products from the market to ensure the stabilisation of prices and maximisation of profits.

Leslie Farris, in a letter to the Guardian, (10/12/1993) writes:

> "Advocates of free trade...are wittingly or unwittingly endorsing the "trickle down" theory of economics on global scale, The few hundred trans-national companies which hog *70% of the world market* [my emphasis. S.T.] are set to increase that percentage as the direct result of the Gatt settlement. In due course they will gobble each other up and monopolies or cartels will develop even further beyond the control of any remotely accountable body. *Such are the immutable laws of the market place* [my emphasis. S.T.]"

b) About 10 years ago, a Nigerian diplomat was kidnapped in London and an attempt was made to return him to Nigeria in a packing case for trial for corruption. It was alleged that he had secreted some £4,000,000 of

public money into a numbered Swiss bank account. It was explained to me personally by one of the kidnappers that this man had 'run' the 'mammies' who controlled the markets. Their practice was to withhold products from the market and keep them in store in order to maintain artificially high prices.

"You call this corruption?" I asked.

"Certainly." was the reply.

"In Europe," I said "this is known as:

C.A.P.

The Common Agricultural Policy of the European Economic Community (EEC).

According to the Annual Report of the Intervention Board, 1992 – 1993[5] for the year 1991:

closing stock of cereals:	631,000 tonnes,
closing stock of beef:	140,799,000 tonnes,
closing stock of butter:	25,729,000 tonnes,
closing stock of SMP products:	6,810,000 tonnes.

As regards productive capacity, this does not take into account *restrictions* on productive capacity in the form of farm quotas etc.. According to a report in the Guardian (21/3/1994):

"As Spring approaches, the first green shoots of wheat

---

5. Published by HMSO – figures for Britain only. Presumably similar figures could obtain for all members of the EEC.

should have been poking through the rich brown soil of the Lincolnshire flatlands. Instead, weeds could soon sprout on fields near Immingham ...More than 100 acres, 15% of [Ted Shepherd's] holding have been taken out of production as part of the UK's contribution to ending Europe's grain surplus due to the Common Agricultural Policy.......Around Britain, 1.4 million acres, on an estimated 30,000 farms, will be "set aside" at a cost well over £200,000,000...Nine hundred civil servants [average wage (say) £20,000 p.a. = £18,000,000 p.a. further yearly addition to the PSBR. S.T.] equipped with latest surveillance technology [how much has that cost per civil servant? S.T.] have been recruited to police the regime......It just doesn't seem to make sense." [said Ted Shepherd]"

As we have seen, though this be madness, there is method in it!

At the end of 1993, *for one year only*, the cost of CAP market support remaining with the Agency amounted to (yet another PSBR) *£1,724,794,000.*

All this in world in which three quarters of the population live below the bread line.

c) According to a report in The Guardian (18/10/1993)

"The government has admitted that the £1,300,000,000 annual subsidy to the nuclear industry is designed to reduce the country's dependence on coal [a prime example of market rigging to make nuclear power competitive – what price the free market? S.T.]...Under rules drawn up during electricity privatisation, the regional companies are *obliged* [my emphasis – free market? S.T.] to buy a fixed amount of their power from more expensive and renewable power sources and are reimbursed through the levy.

"It is to expire in 1998, when it will have contributed £9,100,000,000 to Nuclear Electric (see 'Constituents of the Debt' above)."

This is all in accord with the vendetta against the mining industry by the establishment who have never forgotten or forgiven the defeat of the government by the miners in 1974 (or indeed the initiation and their intransigeance of the general strike in 1926, so cruelly betrayed by the 'Labour' bureaucracy and the Trades Union Congress) and described by Mrs. Thatcher as 'the enemy within' or 'traitors' to justify the equivalent of a military operation against the miners and their families during the 1984 strike. The whole strategy, both during and since the strike has been designed to dismantle and destroy the coal industry, notwithstanding the fact British coal is the cheapest in the world and there are sufficient reserves to sustain Britain's energy needs for the next 400 years.

The details of the secret war against the NUM – the single most ambitious counter-subversion operation ever mounted by the British security services, including a comprehensive intelligence dirty tricks campaign of smear tactics encouraged by an extra-ordinary alliance of interests, including the Conservative Government,

Robert Maxwell, factions of the Labour Party etc etc. – has been documented by the Guardian journalist Seamus Milne in the book 'The Enemy Within' (published by Verso, 6 Meard St, London W1VR 3HR), but the carnage merrily continues.

According to a report in the Guardian (20/10/1992):

> "The government and British Coal yesterday cleared a legal path for a second wave of pit closures which could leave the industry with only 15 deep mines, a larger closure programme than the one Michael Heseltine was forced to withdraw a year ago after a national outcry. Announcement of the plan, which would probably mean cutting a further 10,000 mining jobs.....*has been crafted by ministers to avoid repetition of the nationwide protests.*" [my emphasis. S.T.]

One sure way of winning the 'class war' is to destroy the industry on which the 'class enemy' depends – practical Marxism. The whole affair was openly characterised by leading German industrialists on a BBC Television documentary programme as completely beyond comprehension.

d) Where no market exists, artificial markets are created to ward off the collapse of the market system (despite rigging) as a result of overproduction – the problem of surpluses. This may be characterised as:

Abstract Production:

Can we store some spent nuclear fuel in your greenhouse?

Production for production's sake:

1) Waste and production for waste:

CASE STUDY

The Thorp Nuclear Reprocessing Plant:

According to a report in the Guardian (20/10/1993):–

> "Two potentially fatal blows have been dealt to the controversial £2.3 billion[6] Thorp reprocessing plant at Sellafield by Germany's legal watchdog over State spending and the Irish Government.

> "The German Government has been told by the federal audit court that its multi–million contracts with British Nuclear Fuels, on which the future of Thorp depends, should be cancelled because reprocessing spent fuel is *"economically unviable"* [my emphasis S.T]. It could be twice as expensive as storing the fuel in salt caverns underground....

> "Dublin has now cast doubt on the economic case for Thorp....etc.etc."

The Panorama programme referred to exposed beyond any doubt a comedy of errors, incompetence, and pig-

---

6. This figure was given in a recent BBC Panorama Programme as £2.8 billion, this being the figure quoted in the section 'Constituents of the Debt' above. S.T.

headedness, all objections and clear warnings being cast aside under an astonishing variety of evasions and excuses while, in their determination to proceed, successive Ministers paraded their ignorance on television like a victory .

It is, of course, entirely open to question as to why industries exist at all which result in the production of nuclear waste requiring storing or any sort of reprocessing, and the whole of the nuclear industry itself should be subsumed under the rubric of 'abstract production'. Never mind that it is unprofitable without subsidy – it is not only entirely superfluous, but also comprises a threat to the existence of life (remember Chernobyl, Windscale etc.) on the planet. How many billions of pounds has that added to the PSBR?

Should it have turned out to be profitable as a going concern, this might have been a bonus, but was completely irrelevant to the exercise. The contractors have made a profit, the sub–contractors have made a profit, the manufacturers have made a profit, mechanical and electrical installation companies have made a profit, the consultants have made a profit, etc. etc. and the capitalist mode of production is victorious and rolls merrily on and all at a cost to the public borrowing sector of a mere £2,800,000,000, (a great victory over reason and worth every penny – "it was a good piece of business – three or four times better value than we paid for, as Mrs Tweazle(thatcher) said to her husband when she came home from market" (W. Cobbett)

I would note in passing that I do not hesitate to use the word 'capitalist' when describing the current universally prevailing mode of production. It seems to me the term is unambiguous i.e. production for profit. The relationships of the labour process alone, while an integral part of capitalism (at least as it has existed to the present) are not sufficient to define the system. The relationships of the production process are also necessary. This means the ramifications of meaning contained in the phrase: 'production for profit' –i.e. the accumulation process which (until recently, at any rate) reproduced itself on an ever larger and extended scale. Capitalism is dynamic, a thing of many faces, but only one aim – profit. It should be added that whether this aim is best served by the 'free' wage labourer, or by slavery, or by indented or forced labour of one kind or another, or whether it is conducted in the interests of private property owners, national or multi-national corporations, or the privileged strata of a state bureaucracy (e.g. the now defunct, quadruply misnamed, Union of Soviet Socialist Republics) is irrelevant. It is the failure to recognise this as well as the *deliberate falsification* by demagogues of both left and right, from the various breeds of Stalinist rabble to Mrs. Thatcher and her like, which has so degraded the term 'socialism' and so distorted its associations that its original meaning of 'production for use' has been lost forever.

Returning to Thorp, we find (surprise! surprise!):–

"The new international opposition to Thorp comes at

17

time when BNFL (British Nuclear Fuels) is fighting a fierce battle with its two domestic customers, Nuclear Electric and Scottish Nuclear, over £15 billion of reprocessing and waste contracts including Thorp. The power companies are pushing for price reductions of up to 20%.

"Clive Bates, an economist with Greenpeace, in a letter to Bob Hawley, Nuclear Electric's chief executive[7] said that the two British power companies were pro-posing to pay 200% more for reprocessing than it would cost to store fuel. *The conclusion must therefore be that the large discrepancy is nothing less than a covert subsidy paid to BNFL by the electricity consumer, with Nuclear Electric and Scottish Nuclear merely acting as a conduit'* [My emphasis – *sic transit gloria* from the benefits and panacea of 'open' competition and the 'free (!) market'. S.T.]'"

All this of course is independent of environmental issues, which would require a separate study. Sufficient to note the headline and report: (Observer 24/10/1993):

"New cancer fears raise Minister's fears on Thorp"
"The Government's radioactive waste advisers have received urgent instructions to review alarming new estimates by Government and independent scientists of likely world wide deaths from the Thorp plant at Sellafield ....Officials fear these new concerns ..... could unravel the Government's entire case for approving the

---

7. We don't have 'bosses' any more – they are all CEO's (Chief Executive Officers)

plant. Under the Radioactive Substances Act 1960, every new radioactive discharge must be justified by *demonstrating that economic gains (!) will outweigh (!) the damage (!) to human health (!)* [my emphasis. S.T.].

Such are the equations of the market!

Notwithstanding all the above, it is announced that the government is expected to give the go–ahead for the opening of the plant very soon! (BBC News, 15/12/1993). This immediately commits the taxpayer to a further *£1 billion* for the costs of decommissioning, but, says BNFL, they have orders for over £9 billion on their books, and they expect to make a profit of £500,000,000 over the next ten years (half the cost of decommissioning). This forecast is based on figures and analyses *which have not been made public* (see under "confidentiality" below)".

According to a report in the Guardian: (8/2/1994):

"Greenpeace and Lancashire County Council could not argue their cases [for having the processes which led to the government granting the go–ahead last December declared illegal] on economic viability because *they had been denied information on the contracts with foreign organisations planning to have spent nuclear fuel reprocessed* [just so! my emphasis. S.T.].

According to a further report in The Guardian (3/2/1994):

"The financial uncertainty surrounding British Nuclear Fuels was underlined yesterday when its auditors stamped a health warning on the company's much delayed accounts, citing doubts on the future nearly £17 billion of fuel processing with its two main British customers.....and revealed that if the Government refused to underwrite the huge contracts, the accounts would be "rendered invalid"....The Ernst and Young warning reads: "The company regards such *financial support* in the form of *underwriting* to be a *prerequisite* [my emphasis – *£17 billion* – another PSBR. S.T.] to the completion of these contracts."

Thus what was said above regarding the irrelevance of profit through the market as long as the tax payer will foot the bill is confirmed.

This particular example has been quoted at length because, it encapsulates the total irrationality of the system in which waste and production for waste finds its *ultima ratio* in:

2) Defence:

War and production for war as the mode of existence of post *laissez faire* capitalism.

The armaments industry has implications far beyond the statistics of expenditure and appropriation:

a) The absorption of excess production capacity in overcoming the problem of surpluses and political expediency in maintaining employment levels. It is significant that when, under the whip of absolute necessity, attempts are made to cut military expenditure, one of the biggest howls is concerned with the 'loss of jobs,' especially from the Trades Unions. Unfortunately, there is an increasingly vast segment of the economy which can never again produce consumer goods under capitalism.

Notwithstanding the promised cuts in the defence budget, they cannot escape their destiny, and it comes as no surprise to read a report in The Guardian (24/4/1994) under the headline: Spending on arms '1 bn over the top':

> "Overspending on weaponry for Britain's armed forces has reached nearly £1 billion [another PSBR. S.T.], a report by Parliament's financial watchdog reveals today.

> "Contractors are on average 2.7 years late in delivering the goods, with some of the worst examples – such as the updating of Tornado jets – nearly six years behind schedule."

The inference is so obvious as hardly to need saying – if these updated Tornado jets are so essential for the 'defence of the realm', why have not our potential enemies seized the opportunity and conquered us and delivered us into slavery instead of waiting like idiots for the updating to be completed? This question could have been continually asked during the whole of the 40 years 'cold war' when somehow or other, the Russians always seemed to be 'ahead'. What is said above is confirmed. The end product of the production process is secondary. Production for production's sake *par excellence*!

b) The appropriation of taxpayers money to pay for the unprofitable sectors of armaments production: Major example – Star Wars: billions and billions of dollars shot into space for no good reason but the continued existence of the arms industry at the peoples' expense and the blackmailing of the people to pay for the unprofitable costs of hi–tech research and development from which private industry will eventually reap the profit (if any), but, as noted, this is a secondary consideration.

c) Sponsorship of the policing of the world through direct military intervention and direct and indirect support of State terrorism in the interests of the Metropolitan countries:

Examples

1) The Cold War.

The so–called ideological basis used to justify the arms drive on both sides of the so–called iron curtain reflected the expression of interests in common between East & West rather than opposed, as exemplified by the connivance and support given to the Soviet Union by the West in the barbaric suppression of the uprisings in

Hungary in 1957 and Czechoslovakia in 1968.

Having for years, for propaganda purposes, broad-casting on what they called 'Radio Free Europe', ex-horted the peoples of Eastern Europe daily to rise against their Russian oppressors with voluble assurances of massive aid, every promise was broken – not a finger was lifted to help, not one gesture of political support, not one weapon sent, not one resolution for the Security Council of the United Nations: on the contrary, in Hungary, for example, the puppet regime of the butcher Kadar was recognised by the West before the guns had even stopped firing.

This confirms the view that the Soviet Union, as well as engaging in imperialist depredation on its own behalf all in accordance with the meticulously worked out ar-rangements so carefully prepared at the post-war con-ferences between the 'great allies' at Potsdam, Yalta, Teheran etc., also functioned as capitalism's policeman in Eastern Europe.

According to a letter in The Times, signed by *Bertrand Russell, Jean Paul Sartre, Vladimir Dedijer, and Lauren Schwartz* (9/10/1968):

> "We have reason to believe, on the basis of *prima facie* evidence, that the United States and the Soviet Union are enacting an understanding which involves the recip-rocal support for the crimes of each in its agreed "sphere of influence". This is at the expense of the

independence and self–determination of other nations, from Europe to Vietnam. The secret diplomacy of the rulers of the United States and of the Soviet Union threatens the liberty and sovereignty of men everywhere. It is essential that this *identity of interests* [my emphasis: S.T.] should be fully understood and opposed in the interests of truth."

Notwithstanding, for forty years the barrage of lies about the Russian 'strength' dominated official ideology and propaganda requiring ever widening and deepening involvement in an alleged arms race to 'deter' the Russian war–crazed aggressors, hell bent on world domination, from carrying out their global plans.

The fallacy of the illusion that sufficiently horrible weapons will prevent war has already been amply demonstrated by history (as Alfred Nobel learned to his chagrin, and many a Nobel prize scientist has yet to learn) lies in attributing too great a role to consciousness. To delineate for a patient in the early stages of cancer the horrors of the later stages does not 'deter' the disease from progressing.

It certainly did not 'deter' the U.S. Forces from dropping a greater tonnage of bombs on Vietnam in one day than was dropped in the whole of World War II or the barbaric invasions of Hungary and Czechoslovakia by the Russians or the use of chemical weapons and poison gas obligingly supplied by the West from those bastions of civilisation known as Chemical Weapons Establishments during the Iraq/Iran War by Iraq on the

24

Kurds etc. – the list could be extended indefinitely.

It is diverting to note that the name 'Chemical Weapons Establishment' has proved far too forthright and accurate and likely to offend delicate sensibilities to be acceptable, so this august institution is now officially subsumed under the blanket title: 'Defence Research Association'.

Even with the collapse of the Russian slum empire, despite much prating about the 'peace dividend', the military axis cannot be broken and new 'justifications' magically appear.

Thus we are regaled on the BBC News (27/1/1994) with pictures of extensive Civil Defense operations in South Korea to counter the imminent threat of North Korea's huge nuclear arsenal "in the hands of a mad dictator!" amidst reports of huge North Korean troop movements towards the 'demilitarised' zone between North and South Korea, and the undertaking of extensive military exercises by the Americans in concert with the South Korean army, described by a North Korean spokesman as 'provocative' and a 'threat to the stability of the region' – a curious coincidence with Japan's announcements of increased military spending and America's expressed determination to extend its sphere of influence into Asia.

According to the Guardian (16/11/1993):

"And beyond [NAFTA & GATT] lies the prospect of extending that free trading area into the world's fastest growing region of Asia and the Pacific....So the White House, hoping for a win in the NAFTA vote, has prepared a draft paper for this week's Asia Pacific summit in Seattle which suggests the Pacific rim nations moving forward to PAFTA (Pacific American Free Trade Area) on their own."

And pat on cue comes a report in The Economist (November 6–12/11/1993):

"The passing of the cold war, which helped to change Japan's politics, is also changing its defence policy. On October 31st. the prime minister, Morihiro Hasokaw said Japan should speed up a review of its security which had been due for completion by 1995. The next day, Les Aspen, America's Defence Secretary arrived in Japan to talk about *the new enemies which had replaced the faded Russian threat* [my emphasis. S.T.]"

Thus, according to The Guardian (16/11/1993):

"With tension on the Korean peninsula at its highest for years because of North Korea's alleged nuclear ambitions, troops from the United States and South Korea began ten days of joint exercises today which Pyongyang said could lead to war. The exercises, codename Foldeagle, are designed to test how South Korea could cope with aggression from the North."

One way or another the mighty war machines must be kept rolling and the public bombarded with justification ideologies.

What is involved has been set out by Naom Chomsky[8]

"A principle familiar to propagandists is that the doctrine to be instilled in the target audience should not be articulated; that would only expose them to reflection, inquiry, and very likely, ridicule. The proper procedure is to drill them home by constantly presupposing them so that they become the very condition of discourse. The technique is illustrated nicely in Nigel Gordon's front page *News of the Week and Review* story in the *New York Times* headlined "Greater Threat from Lesser Powers: The Middle East's Awful Arms Race." The opening sentence sets the framework; "With the Soviet military threat (?) receding, the spread of chemical, biological, and nuclear weapons to the Third World [dropping there like manna from heaven, no doubt S.T.] is fast emerging as the greatest danger to the stability of the world." This statement presupposes what we are to understand as a truism: in the past, the Soviet military threat has been the greatest danger to "stability" (a good thing). Now, we are informed, advanced weaponry in the Third World is replacing it......

So it is the Muslim world who are responsible for "The Middle East's Awful Arms Race". The proliferation threat is becoming "awful" *now*, not thirty years ago when France helped Israel build its Dimona nuclear

---

8. Letters from Lexington – Reflections on Propaganda, (published AK Press, Edinburgh) in a letter dated 15th April, 1990.

reactor and in violation of its pledge Israel began to use heavy water provided by Norway. Then the United States [turned a blind eye when] Israel began to produce nuclear weapons there. Similarly, the threat to peace is *Iraq's* effort to obtain high speed switches to trigger nuclear bombs, *not* the smuggling of the same devices to Isreal years earlier by Los Angeles business man Robert Smythe.......

One essential point is a tolerance for contradiction. Thus Patrick Tyler observes that "Gaps remain in the administration's goal of slimming the Middle East arms race, even as Washington has become the dominant arms supplier in the region."......The administration's goal is to stem the Middle East arms race is Truth established by assertion from on high. Washington's explanation of the opportunity to sell hi-tech weapons is mere fact, too insignificant to undermine Truth....Fact is merely the abuse of reality – Truth is reality itself."

2) Complicity in Gangsterism.

As is well known from Hollywood movies, gangsters will shoot each other quite cheerfully and engage in gang wars (elimination of competitors who have become 'dangerous'), but, under the pressure of circumstances, know very well how to combine against any threat which is too large for any single gang to handle, i.e. the threat to gangsterism itself:

Examples:

a) The Russian Army at the gates of Warsaw. Under the direct orders of Stalin, having called the underground to arms with voluble and encouraging promises of massive help, the Russian army looked on while German SS units slaughtered the heroic Polish resistance. Warsaw, the first European capital to be reached in World War 2, was the last to be 'liberated'.

b) Complicity in the quelling of the Czechoslovakian and Hungarian uprisings as cited above.

c) The Gulf War: having gained their strategic aim of securing their oil supplies, what the 'allies' (read Americans) would have tolerated was a palace coup (a revolt of the army to replace Hussein without altering the status quo) – what they got was a popular revolt – Shiites in the South, Kurds in the North, and the heroic Iraqi Democratic Front (who had been opposing Hussein and suffering for it for years, but never even got a mention in the press). Gangsterism itself threatened: Response – The Americans, having brutally slaughtered a retreating and desperate conscript rabble trying only to get home (operation Desert Storm), stopped at the border to allow their good friend Saddam Hussein to deal with the real revolution (in an area where their other policeman, Israel, had been forbidden to intervene because the Americans did not want to alienate their Arab 'allies') and pursue his genocidal policies without restraint – a danger spot eliminated.

3) Market-in-itself:

Supply of arms to reactionary and genocidal regimes: Indonesia, Israel, Iraq, etc.. Sub-plot: Israel in its turn supplying arms to bolster the most reactionary regime in the world, South Africa, to 'defend' apartheid.

The complicity of the Government in the supply of arms to Indonesia for pursuing their genocidal policies in East Timor was exposed by John Pilger in his fine February television documentary, and the complicity of the West, especially Britian, in the supply of arms to Iraq up to within days of the Gulf War behind a smokescreen of disinformation, lies, and cover-ups, seeps into the newspapers daily through the revelations of the Scott enquiry. These phenomena would need a separate study to do them justice, but it is worth remarking that great indignation was manifest by the opposition at the trial of the directors of Matrix Churchill on the ground that the Government had tried to prevent the courts hearing evidence which clearly showed that they were 'innocent', as if any persons who manufacture and supply arms to brutal and ruthless dictators carrying out genocidal policies could possibly be described as 'innocent'.

One attempt to prevent the revelations by the Government through an injunction was refused by the courts, since, as the judge remarked, what was wanted would have reversed the English Revolution of the 17th century!

4) Back-handers

Public moneys are appropriated to finance deals in the international arms trade through foreign 'aid' (I cannot omit the quotes) programme.

> "John Major personally overruled Whitehall's top aid expert to fund a "bad buy" Malaysian power station that helped to underpin a controversial aid–for–arms deal agreed by Lady Thatcher...Lady Thatcher was ...known to have promised the Malaysian Government that Britain would help the project in return for Malaysia's placing lucrative arms and trade orders – [abstract production – an unwanted and unprofitable hydro–electric power station with who knows what environmental implications. S.T.] engendering further abstract production i.e. arms deals! S.T.]...Sir Tim [Lankaster] revealed that Mr Major had overruled a memorandum warning that Britain's biggest aid package for the Pergau hydro–electric power station was "unequivocally a bad one in economic terms" [for whom? for the builders of the damn? for the arms dealers? Oh! for the taxpayer – tut! tut! S.T.]" and "an abuse of the aid programme [wrong! – this is the essence of *all* 'aid' programmes. S.T.]" MP's were told that *ministers had refused them access to the full text of the memorandum outlining Sir Tim's objections.* [Quite so! my emphasis. S.T.] (Guardian 18/1/1994)

Watchword (as noted above): **There is no sentiment in business:**

> "The United Nations is expected to vote next month on

31

a world wide ban on the export of anti–personnel mines
to stamp out a trade that had left 100,000,000 uncleared
land mines in 56 countries, killing perhaps thousands of
civilians each week. The export ban...is opposed by the
British government *which does not want to lose its
share of a valuable export market.*[my emphasis S.T.]
Britain is trying to fend off the ban by proposing a
conference to discuss the problem [for whom? S.T.]
(Sunday Times – Oct.1993)

Confidentiality:

**Claimed by the State as an inalienable right 'in the
public or national interest', this is the cover phrase
for the fact that governments only keep things from
the public because they are so diabolical and go-
vernments are so afraid of the consequences that
they dare not let the public get a whiff of them.**

*This is true of all secret negotiations, classified
information, withholding of information or refusing to
make documents available etc.*

Example: The Spycatcher affair, where top civil ser-
vants admitted lying their heads off but which the
whole world was allowed to read except the British
public – a matter of principle – the principle of
'confidentiality' said Mrs Thatcher.

New aphorisms, or perhaps, euphemisms have been
added to the language: 'disinformation': civil servants
may be 'economical with the truth' and anything goes

so long as there is 'plausible deniability' – i.e. we will lie our heads off as long as you can't prove we are doing so!

Anyway, the Scott enquiry has done away with the need for euphemisms? We are now told that Ministers have the *right* to lie! Under the headline "Uproar over 'right to lie'" The Guardian (9/3/1994) reports:

> "The cabinet minister responsible for open government [!], William Waldegrave, provoked a fresh storm over Government contempt for parliament when he told MP's yesterday that it was sometimes right for ministers to lie to the Commons...etc., etc.,etc."

The new Official Secrets Act was purported to have loosened the rules etc., but the fact remains that a programme transmitted on television on a certain Monday regarding MI5 & MI6 had become illegal by the following Thursday. The defence of 'in the public interest' was wiped from the statute books.

This all touches on the political parameters of the PSBR, and the constant erosion of our civil rights currently being enshrined in the new Criminal Justice Act within the framework of a developing totalitarianism, including the abolition of the 'right to silence' and the criminalisation of demonstrations through new trespass laws, etc.etc., a major cause for concern, but the detailed investigation of which would require a separate study.

Enterprise Culture:

The framework of financial avarice and manipulation (swindling of the people),: a usurers charter[9]permitting and encouraging the exploita-

---

9) Userer's Charter – A Case Study

12th December 1990: Loan from Finance Company: £27,000

19th February 1991: Communication from Finance Company:–

Because you wish to settle your agreement early, we are *required* [my emphasis. S.T.] to calculate the total interest you would have paid if the agreement had continued to its full term and deduct from this an Interest Rebate calculated in accordance with the Consumer Credit Act (Rebate on Early Settlement) Regulations 1983.

Outstanding balance as at 12th. February, 1991:	£26,291.88
Future Interest which you would have paid:	28,896.37
Total amount repayable before any rebate:	55,818.25
Less: Rebate	27,304.61
Settlement Amount	28,513.64
Plus Discharge Fee	34.50
Amount required to discharge valid to Settlement Date:	£28,548.14

(which has been calculated in accordance with Regulation 3 of the Consumer Credit (Settlement Information) Regulation 1983)......

Settlement Date: 12 March 1991 [3 months after date of loan: S.T.]

Sgnd........

Note: To the above figure must be added the amount of loan repaid from 12/12/1992 – 12/3/1993: i.e.	£ 1,200.66
Total (which would have been paid to Finance Company had debt been settled):	£29,748.80

34

tion of market forces for private gain.

"Gravity–defying City salaries are expected under the political spotlight following the revelation that an arbitrage dealer operating in the financial markets earned(!?) £9,000,000 last year....The dictionary defines arbitrage as 'simultaneously buying something in one market and selling it in another. In economics this term usually applies to buying and selling the currencies of two or more countries in different markets.'

"Despite the huge rewards, true arbitrage is not speculative and is relatively risk free.....[my emphasis. S.T.]

"Mr Alimouti is unlikely to enjoy being the centre of attention...[hardly surprising – S.T.] (but) his success (does not) appear to have aroused professional jealousy. 'He is a pussy cat....' was one verdict last night." (Guardian, 28/10/1993)

However, it would appear that the pussy cat is in fact a pauper!

"Graham Kirkham, chairman of the furniture group

Less: Original Loan	27,000.00
i.e. Interest payable over 3 months:	2,748.80

This represents an annual interest rate of **40.72%**   A usurer's charter indeed!

DFS, laid claim to the title of Britain's highest–paid business man with the revelation that the company paid him more than £20,000,000 in emoluments and dividends in 1992/93. (Guardian, 28/10/1993)

The man's a fraud! He has no right to make such a claim.

"Peter Wood, the Chief executive of Direct Line, is expected to receive a one–off payment of £50,000,000 [in addition to a remuneration of £18,000,000 S.T.] this week in a deal with the telephone–only insurance company's parent, The Royal Bank of Scotland..... the one–off payment appears to be a very good deal for Mr Wood [you bet! S.T.] and Royal Bank shareholders [together, hopefully, with the entire population of Britain S.T.] are certain to question how it can be justified. [Guardian 22/11/1993]

But not, of course, the government, who question nothing, but insist that taxation *must* be related to spending, *not* income, but not, of course, government spending (see 'constituents of the debt' above).

This stance is justified by Kenneth Clarke, Chancellor of the Exchequer, on the ground that indirect taxation is fair because the rich spend more than the poor and therefore pay more taxes. This is tantamount to saying that a tax on spending is *in fact* a tax on income, but even a Chancellor of the Exchequer should be able to realise that the proportion of income spent by low and middle income earners on fuel is far higher than that spent by Mr. Wood.

According to the Low Pay Unit, the % rise in the cost of living for lower paid families after the introduction of VAT on fuel would be up to £175 per week would be 1.09. The equivalent rise for Mr. Wood, even with his many mansions, swimming pools, etc., etc., would be in the region .001%.

Again, according to the Guardian (6/4/1994):

> "...the richest 1% – some 262,000 people – *will hardly notice the extra tax burden* [my emphasis. S.T.] since they are on an average £325 *better off* [my emphasis. S.T.] than in 1989 and have been largely untouched by the recession. Their taxable income has on average risen by £317,238 per year.
>
> The top 5 & 10% of taxpayers – about 2.6 million people have also done well....They are, on the whole, between £40 and £78 a week better off in cash terms than in 1989."

In any case, isn't there just a nice little loophole in the law whereby the rich could avoid paying the tax anyway – they simply bought years' supply of electricity etc., in advance *before* the law came into effect!

Fair shares for all, but some shares are fairer than others!

If Mr. Clarke was right and all taxes on spending

actually related all taxation proportionately to income in the same proportion as the taxation of lower income earners, the PSBR would simply disappear overnight, but, in the event, no attempt is made to counteract the kind of money manipulation (at which Mr Wood and his ilk are so adept) known as:

TAX EVASION:

Manipulation of tax rules to avoid paying taxes – budget policy: shush! not a word!

Under the headline: "£1bn tax loopholes aid Tory backers'", The Guardian reports (3/11/1993):

> " Parliamentary answers given in July suggest that as many as 100,000 people [paupers every one – they will really suffer from the new VAT rules on fuel! S.T.] benefit from confused (?) rules on UK residence and nationality. They might save an average of £20,000 a year, leading to a total tax loss of *£2,000,000,000* [? – why did the headline writer state '£1bn'? S.T,]..."

On the other hand, for example, the 'non–wealth creating sectors' of society such as education and health are appropriately rewarded – the average pay of nurses is £192.70 per week (£10,020 per annum) and of teachers is £380.20 per week (£19,770 per annum), and *no pay rises are to be awarded this year;* i.e. taking into account inflation this effectively amounts to a *cut* in salary (at the moment when the *weekly* increase in salary awarded to Lord Young, of the 'sweeteners' (read 'gifts' from the privateers...etc) to BAe. fame, Chairman of Cable and Wireless) is greater than the total *yearly* salary of, e.g., a care assistant employed by a Local Authority [10] – a true gift from the privateers of Britain to one of their number). While public sector employees are limited a pay rise of 2% (of what? – actual figures are seldom reported, but it is sure that nurses will indulge in unbridled rejoicing at the prospect of a pay rise of £3.85 per week) the Guardian reports (18/6/1994):

"Top directors have received pay rises averaging 25% in the past year despite repeated calls for boardroom moderation against a back–ground of low inflation. Salary increases for leading business men include a 200% rise for Peter Wood [that pauper again! S.T.] whose pay last year toped £18,000,000 [am mere £700,000 rise *per week*. S.T.] .....etc. etc."

Since writing this, the Government appeared to have bowed to public pressure and announced a 3% rise in salary for teachers, but *no extra money* has been allocated for this purpose which, it is stated, has to be found from increased efficiency. This can only mean one thing. Loss of jobs and increase in the size of classes. As though to order comes a headline in the Observer (6/3/1994): "Patten [Minister of Education] Plans to Close 1,000 Schools." When it comes to the PSBR, it's all, of course, a matter of priorities.

So the people are robbed. Press on – VAT on fuel, means testing,

---

10. All figures from the Low Pay Unit.

cutting the income of the less well off, cutting old age pensions, income support, housing benefit, the NHS, public services, cut, cut, cut, etc. etc.

No sooner had these words been written than the following headline appeared in the Sunday Times (5/12/1993): "Extracting tax by a thousand cuts!" and in the body of the article it shows that:−

"£25,000 earners [lucky people − in work. Better paid than nurses or teachers. S.T.] will find their income reduced by 3.39% whereas £75,000 earners (?) will find themselves 1.9% worse off."

According to the Guardian (14/1/1994):

"The combined effect of Mr. Lamont's March budget and Kenneth Clarke's November budget committed the present government to the biggest tax increase in post war history, − *£7.9 billion this coming spring and a cumulative £15 billion in 1995.* [my emphasis: S.T.]

and again: (Guardian 6/4/1994):

...official figures [were released yesterday] showing many of Britain's poorest taxpayers will be paying for today's tax rises from pay packets smaller that 4 years ago....The pay figures, released by the Treasury Financial Secretary, Stephen Dorrell, show that the bottom 50% of taxpayers − who face higher national insurance contributions, VAT on fuel, and reduced tax allowances − are on the average already £4.50 a week worse off than in 1989 because of reduced overtime and lower pay.

Their average pay fell by £10 per week between 1989 and 1991...[so much for Mrs Thatcher's 'trickle down' effect. S.T.]"

In other words – starve yourselves to greatness as the Prussians did of old, or, as they say in Russia,: "AY DA OOCH NIEM (Yo ho, heave ho)!" without end, whether on the dole or not!

Under the headline "Welfare state eyed by insurers – Industry identifies big opportunities", The Guardian (22/10/1993) reports:

"Insurance industry chiefs are drawing up plans to "cherry pick" parts of the welfare state in preparation for the *privatisation* [my emphasis S.T.] of large tracts of the health and social security services...The insurers have identified areas where they see opportunities in taking over welfare state functions.

– Collaboration and joint ventures with the NHS to help reduce the £37 billion budget for 1993/1994.

– Expansion of private medical insurance beyond the current 6.5 million policy holders, either through fiscal incentives to the under 60's or through a contracting out system of certain NHS benefits.

– The provision of long term care for the elderly, possibly through tax–assisted (!) release of equity tied up in property estimated to be worth £400 billion (!!!)1.25

– The transfer of liability for industrial injury, social security and invalidity to employers, currently costing the state £7 billion.

– Private unemployment insurance. State jobless benefits are due to cost £10.4 billion next year.

– Contracting out of the state pensions, which currently costs 26.6 billion.

"Mark Boleat, the ABI'S (Association of British Insurers) director–general said: 'I would not call it cherry picking.....

Indeed not, but then life is, after all, just a bowl of cherries.

This comprises a package of £480 billion in pickings due to be handed over by the privateers of England to the privateers of England.

It is built into the nature of things that the virtual privatisation of the welfare state announced by Peter Lillee (the doubly misnamed minister for (anti)Social (in)Security – see footnote 2 above) – will devolve the running and ownership of the these matters to the insurance companies who have provided Peter Wood and his like with their modest income.

The Government is obviously in love with the private sector, BUT – the course of true love never did run smooth.

After endorsement of the notion of handing over the Welfare State to the Insurance companies (at exactly the moment when this policy is being reversed in that model of 'socialist' planning, America) by both Peter

Lillie and John Major, we read in the Observer (12/12/93):–

> "The latest in series of insurance blunders (?) raise doubts about industry plans to take over chunks of the welfare state...The Securities and Investments Board has confirmed shortcomings in the advice [ha!ha!] given to many of the 500,000 people who have moved £7 billion from employers to personal pensions...they may (?) have been conned (tut!tut!)....but insurers are convinced further private welfare provision is inevitable....Some confirmation of this came on Friday with publication of a Department of Social Security (?) document....[What's a £7 billion scam between friends? S.T.]...."

and pat to hand comes a comforting message from Mr. Portillo (Chief Secretary to the Treasury and personally responsible for orchestrating the Poll Tax fiasco which poured £3.5 billion of tax–payers money down the drain). Under the headline "Portillo predicts big welfare cuts" the Guardian reports (25/10/1993):

> "[Speaking on] BBC TV's On the Record, Michael Portillo suggested; "The State should not be relied on for health services and welfare where people could make their own provision [through insurance companies, of course. S.T.]...Should it [the demand on the State. S.T.] get any bigger, it is going to impose such a burden on the wealth creating sector of this country it is going to crush it."

We will return to this gem in due course.

Inflation:

The withering away of the purchasing power of money in the interests of short term profitability through the continuous increase in the differential between cost of production and price at the cost of long term uncompetitiveness.

Decreases in the costs of production (through the introduction of technology or manipulation of tariffs etc.) are never matched proportionately by decreases in price.

Example:

The recent disclosure of the exorbitant retail selling price of compact discs and the resultant astronomical profit levels when compared with the costs of production described by Gerald Kaufman, Chairman of the House of Commons National Heritage Select Committee during the televised proceedings of the Enquiry into the Costs of Compact Discs as "a complete rip-off." Notwithstanding, it is, of course, instructive to note that the price of CD's has not been reduced by one penny.

A glowing report of the beneficial effect of the proposed tariff cuts in the GATT talks (Observer, 12/12/1993) states:

In some sectors, such as electronics, tariffs are to be slashed by as 65% (sic!), and in others, including steel, some tariffs will disappear. The obvious (?) upshot of such a large cut in rates should be a general reduction in shop prices... *In practice, however, markets are not that simple....*[my emphasis S.T].

Prices only fall as demanded by the processes of competition – the need to eliminate competitors.

When the *'I or You'* of *lassez faire* competition becomes the *'We or You'* of Industrial Monopoly Capitalism, there is no extreme which is unthinkable in the elimination of competitors which have become dangerous. Do we not have two massive establishment bloodlettings (known as World Wars I & II) *and* nuclear bombs to prove it?

The need to reduce prices under the aegis of competition is contained by the processes of monopolisation (inherent in the process of the elimination of competitors) and cartelization (see 'market forces' above), thus *restricting* production in the interest of keeping prices high and *creating* the situation of 'too much money chasing too few goods'. When extended to the sale of the means of production, the combined process inexorably and continuously raises the cost structure of the economy – costs of means of production assume a greater and greater proportion of the costs of production, which inflationary *result* of maximising profits through cartelisation is transformed by its apologists into the *cause* of inflation.[11]/[12].

It is, of course, unthinkable to contemplate that inflation could be counteracted by increasing the volume of goods being chased by the money thus bringing about tendency towards the virtual coincidence of cost of production and price and the disappearance of profit – a circumstance exacerbated by the ever increasing proportion of production costs tied up in costs of the means of production.

This is called by economists 'the tendency of the rate of profit to fall' and was recognised and searchingly analysed by David Ricardo in his magnum opus: The Principles of Political Economy and Taxation, published in 1817.

It is counteracted by the expansion of the range of the

---

17. It can be categorically that all statistics regarding inflation or the rate of inflation etc. are unmitigated rubbish. The three main necessities of the continuation of life are housing, clothing and feeding. The cost of housing rose 700% between 1973 and 1989, *but nowhere is this reflected in any statistic on inflation.*

18. In the middle of the 18th century, Oliver Goldsmith in his poem 'The Deserted Village' described the preacher as 'passing rich on £40 per year.' While this might be considered a slightly ironical assessment, the current *minimum* stipendiary for preachers is, according to the Church Commissioners, £12,200. per annum. Do economists seriously expect us to believe that this equivalence is entirely due to the printing of too much money?

market. The absorption of the rest of the world by Europe into the market economy (accompanied, naturally, by the blessings of Christianity) constitutes the most ruthless, brutal, barbarous, and bloody imposition in the history of mankind,

We are thus faced with the problem of overproduction, unsaleable surpluses and of the saturation of the market[13] (see CAP above). It seems fairly elementary that if the amount of money in circulation could purchase the total amount of commodities on the market, i.e. if selling prices equalled the cost of production, profit would simply evaporate, and simple exchange would take its place – good–bye capitalism!. It is therefore attempted to stabilise the situation under the policy of:

monetarism[14]:

Credo: The prime object of government is *not* (no

---

13. In the peculiar language of economics, the word surplus refers only to the requirements or capacity of the market. It by no means refers to surplus in the sense of more than sufficient to satisfy human need.

14. Mrs Thatcher always insisted that monetarism is *not* a "theory". She was, of course, quite right. It was a prescriptive policy procedure designed to concretise and realise the famous *theoretical* formulation of Marx that under capitalism, the rich will get richer while the poor get poorer – can it then be said that Mrs Thatcher and her colleagues were practising Marxists?

longer)[15] to maintain full employment but to fight inflation through control of money supply –i.e. to drive down the standard of living – "If it isn't hurting, it isn't working." John Major (Prime Minister) – weapon: high interest rates [note: axiom op. cit: – currency manipulation = robbery of the people]: result – low return on capital invested = disincentive for investment: result of the result: massive bankruptcies and destruction of British industry: result of the result of the result: mass unemployment – both open and covert – as deliberate government policy.

This is in sharp contradistinction to the much proclaimed (some years ago) 'right to work', which led Joseph Weber to observe:

> "In capitalist democracy, the 'right to work' is proclaimed without considering whether there are sufficient jobs or whether these will be lost through crises, rationalisation, restriction of production etc. This abstract 'claim' to work reduces itself in practice at best to the tautology that everybody has the right to work if – there *is* work, that is to say, *capitalist* work, not any useful work merely, but of a kind which, under the

---

15. Gone are the halcyon days of the Heath administration when the Chief Secretary to the Treasury could explain "that the objectives of government are simple and aim at raising the standards of living of all sections of the community as quickly as possible." Guardian, circa 1973 (unfortunately the date of the cutting I have is not noted).

laws of competition, yields *profit* to employers or serves to maintain the profit system in the interests of the entirety of employers. The form corresponding to the capitalist 'right to work' is *competition*, for not only does it regulate the number of jobs, but also (competition of employers and competition of workers among themselves for available jobs) the level of wages . In the exact sense, therefore, the right to work amounts to the 'right' of competing with other workers for their jobs in the course of which workers are quite entitled to ruin each other, as are the 'free' employers (every have–not is a potential employer and has the 'right' to open an armaments factory tomorrow if – he owns capital)"[16]

It is thus easy to envisage why 'in the face of determined opposition', Chancellor Kohl of Germany moved with such swiftness for German reunification, destroying the aspirations of the long suffering East Germans at one stroke with the greeting, in the words of a cover to the magazine 'Private Eye': "Welcome to freedom, democracy, and liberty – you're fired!"[17].

---

16. Contemporary Issues, Vol.3, No.10.

17. In reply to a question in the House of Commons, Gillian Shepherd (Minister of (un)Employment) stated: "The young lady will know that I am deeply concerned about the personal hardship of unemployed people and their feelings" (Hansard, 1/12/1992) – The only possible response to this has come from Lewis Carroll (Alice in Wonderland):–

> 'I weep for you,' the walrus said,
> 'I deeply sympathise.'

The manipulation of the labour force and the creation of the pool of unemployed to drive down wages through competition for available jobs is inevitably accompanied by the destruction of the social mechanisms set in place after years of bitter struggle and designed to fix the price of that most controversial of all commodities: labour power.

Practical Marxism indeed. Will Hutton, writing in the Guardian 9/5/1994) observes:

"The Conservatives are the world's first new Marxist party. Only Marxists this century have been so profoundly attached to the labour theory ....That British Conservatives are perversely reclaiming Marxist truths and 'practise' [my quotes. S.T.[18]] as their own is richly

---

With sobs and tears he sorted out
Those of the largest size,
Holding his pocket handkerchief
Before his streaming eyes.

'O oysters,' said the carpenter,
'You've had a pleasant run.
Shall we be trotting home again?'
But answer came there none,
And this was scarcely odd because
They'd eaten every one.

18. How such practice can be described as 'Marxist' it is difficult to fathom, when Marx's specific object was 'the withering away of the state'. A more accurate designation would have been 'Marxist–Leninist' or 'Stalinist'. There is whole school of (post)–

ironic [no – deliberate: the expression of market forces S.T.].

"There two aspects of the party's new neo–Marxism. The first is the belief that efficient capitalism demands the pauperisation of labour – because, like Marx, the Conservatives [rightly S.T.] view ever cheaper labour as the source of all profit and competitiveness. This implies the abandonment of regulation of the labour market and the de facto emasculation of trades unions to allow capital to bid down the price of labour. Thus is the economy made competitive.

"The second aspect is to ensure that all state institutions are commanded by the party and none escape its injunctions.

"Turning its back on the old Burkean anxiety to defend the small platoons of society, in fear that they may embody irrational values hostile to the imperatives of the market, the Conservative centralists have centralised power to maximise the labour value of production for the lowest price. Intermediate institutions ranging from

---

modern French philosophers who are manifesting a renewed interest in Kant and his 'unknowable' thing–in–itself (market forces?) and consider Marx entirely discredited. The answer can only be: 'Tell that to the 5 million unemployed, to the homeless, to those whose earnings have been halved, living below the breadline , caught in the poverty trap, etc.' The point about these people is that if you prick them. they do not bleed. They simply drop another footnote (not that this little homily is short on same!)

local authorities to regional health authorities have either been denuded of competence or re-organised according to market principles. Fragmentation, disintegration and atomisation of society has resulted, overwhelming any localised gains in economic efficiency."

As stated above, inflation is endemic in the nature of competition and it follows that, contrary to carefully inculcated received wisdom to the effect that wage rises cause inflation, the continual struggle is to try and upgrade wage rises *in line* with inflation, notwithstanding temporary gains of one sort or another.

The notion that the mechanisms set up by capitalism to settle the price of labour power (Trades Unions, Labour Parties, and the like) in the market would of themselves generate the political consciousness required to transform society remains a major theoretical error of political Marxism, or is at least historically obsolete, and discussion of which is not relevant here. We may also leave undecided the question as to whether a class that prior to its seizure of power, had neither developed its own mode of production nor exercised any other leading functions, is at all capable of assuming leadership, especially in the light of the reification of these 'so-called' worker's institutions.

Nowhere in the last few years has the absorption of the so-called opposition into the mechanisms of rule been more blatant than in the behaviour of the Labour Party over the poll tax. No measure ever introduced by government has commanded less support or roused more hostility. So unpopular was it that it led to the rejection of Mrs. Thatcher as leader of the Conservatives and as Prime Minister. If such pressure from below could overturn the Tory leadership, there is no doubt whatsoever that it could have swept the Tories from power.

Instead, however, of reflecting the mood of the people and giving their need encouraging and adequate support by *active* and imaginative opposition, by openly supporting the resistance movement against the tax, by non–co–operation with the government and a defiant refusal to implement the legislation and impose the tax, as well to support non–payers, all as befits a true opposition, Labour councils through out the country obediently spent billions of pounds enforcing the legislation, combing electoral registers to track down non–payers, and then prosecuting them. Result; over 4,0000,000 people (potential labour voters every one) failed to register for the electoral role to avoid paying the tax and lost their vote – a more than sufficient margin to have guaranteed electoral victory.

The fact that the Conservatives are still in government can be seen as the direct responsibility of the behaviour of the Labour Party.

This bureaucracy is not only an additional vampire (that is by no means the worst!) but it also ruins the elementary mass movements, poisons the consciousness of many individuals and bolsters up the system at the point where, on account of its brutality and senselessness, it would be most highly vulnerable, from the dissolution of the soviets and the crushing of the Kronstadt revolt in Russia by Lenin and Trotsky, the betrayal of the 1926 general strike in Britain by the TUC and the Labour Party, the behaviour of the Stalinists in Spain in 1936 and the disarming of the resistance movements in Europe after the war to the undermining and destruction of the French revolution of 1968, where the opportunism of the 'left' knew no bounds, diverting the revolutionary energy of the people into sterile economism (adding the sous to the franc) and electoral channels. The following assertion is no literary exaggeration: the modern misery is the work of the Labour bureaucracy.

It is a tenfold misfortune for the working masses that in the course of selling and buying back their labour power (the buying back occurs through the acquisition of the means of subsistence which, as a general rule restores ever less than the average expended labour power), those middlemen who are known under this collective name of 'the Labour bureaucracy', have to be added to all their other burdens.

It is an axiom that capital will follow its interests at any cost, and the manufacturers of the means of production and investors therein look to the widest markets. The costs of production of the means of production rise progressively due to the inflationary process, and the need, therefore of competition can only be satisfied by looking for savings in the cost of labour power (the producer of all values). Thus monetarism, while requiring high interest rates supposedly to control inflation, resulting in a low return (often zero or less the zero – hence the spate of bankruptcies) for capital invested and thus a disincentive for investment, still requires that investment will go where the labour is cheapest and these two objectives are achieved by the deregulation, and with it, the flight of capital – the first act of the Thatcher administration: result: the death knell of British industry.

The export of capital, in its turn, creates hi–tech industry elsewhere with which British industry itself cannot compete[19], and the disappearance of the industrial sector follows as night follows day.

Especially telling is a report on The Observer (24/4/1994) under the headline: "Short–sighted investors add to training failures!"

"Alarm signals about the decline of manufacturing and Britain's long term ability to pay its way in the world are to be issued by two Conservative dominated committees this week...

"A...report to be issued by the Science and Technology

---

19. With pin–point accuracy a banner at a recent miner's protest read:–"MY HOME IS IN DERBY, MY JOB IS IN TAI–WAN."

Committee reinforces the Trade and Industry Committee's call for better investment in research and development and improved finance for small high–tec enterprises. Both committees attack the short term attitudes that dominate so much of British investment and management.

"But the Trade and Industry's report also *challenges government claims that an economy built on low wages is more competitive. That attitude is condemned as shortsighted because skill bolsters productivity, and high output **reduces** unit labour costs! (my emphasis. S.T.)* "

The argument is, of course, completely circular. The 'reduction of unit labour costs' implies the assertion of the law of the tendency of the rate of profit to fall – (more goods for the same amount of labour specifically means an increase in the proportion of the costs of the means of production in the costs of production itself) which it is attempted to counter–act by the expansion of the market itself, and, lo and behold, we are right back with the problem of unsaleable surplusses!

We may note in passing that the government continually points to the fact that, having achieved low rates of inflation, for which, according to Norman Lamont, ex–Chancellor of the Exchequer, mass unemployment was 'a price well worth paying', and concomitantly the virtual destruction of the industrial sector through the path of stagnation, it proudly points to the fact that it has been able to lower interest rates and presages an accompanying consumer led 'recovery'.

The little problem is, and *here, here,* therefore, lies the difficulty, as Cobbett might have said, that, having destroyed the British consumer industry (try buying, eg. a cast iron bath made in Britain or, indeed, any other of a thousand everyday consumer products) the 'consumer' is forced to buy imports from abroad leading to a balance of payments crisis which will, inexorably, force interest rates *up.*

This, it is supposed, will be counteracted by a rise in exports fuelled by the favourable exchange rate for sterling as a result of the devaluation of sterling on Black Wednesday, BUT, after a promising start, this too appears to have ground to a halt because of recession (saturation of the market etc.) in Europe.

According to a report in the Guardian (1/4/1994):

"All the ingredients for a classic run on sterling are now in place, with a configuration of economic and political circumstances attracting the attention of the carnivores in the city [perhaps Mr Alimouti (see under "Enterprise Culture") will be in a position to supplement his meagre income. S.T.]. The pound has fallen steadily for the last couple of months [certainly one of the consequences of low interest rates which renders sterling unattractive to speculators. S.T.] and is at its lowest for almost a year.......Recent data from the Central Statistical Office has started to concentrate minds in the financial markets on the state of Britain's current account. The figures make sorry reading. Even with the economy barely out of recession (?), the trade gap has started to widen alarmingly....The final straw could be a dodgy set of trade figures or an unexpected pick-up in the underlying rate of inflation, since that would increase the prospects of an increase in interest rates."

Those damned *market forces* raising their ugly heads *again,* and, as if to order, comes a report in the Guardian (26/5/1994) under the headline:

"Inflation fears hit markets!

"More than 15 billion was wiped off the value of the London Stock market yesterday as fears that German interest rates may have bottomed out triggered a slump in European share and bond markets.

"In evidence to MP's, Eddie George, the governor of the Bank of England, tried to calm the markets as they showed growing anxiety about higher global inflation....but a sharp decline in the price of government bonds yesterday spilled over into equities, *with the London market witnessing one of its biggest falls since sterling left the Exchange Rate Mechanism.....*

"After the market closed last night, the National Institute of Economic and Social Research – a think tank headed by one of the Chancellors "wise men" [especially the quotation marks! S.T.] called for interest rates to be *increased* [my emphasis. S.T.] by one percentage point to head off a rise in inflation."

Again (Guardian (17/6/1994):

"Market nervy after Chancellor echoes rate rise warning"

And again (Guardian – 21/4/1994)

"£12bn wiped off shares in City panic;

"More than £12 billion was wiped off share values in the City yesterday as financial markets around the world were hit by fears of higher interest rates, higher commodity prices [what price inflation under control? S.T.] and a plunging dollar."

And *again* (Guardian – 25/6/1994)

"Crash wipes £16bn off share values.

"Almost £16 billion was wiped off share values in the City yesterday as a week of global turmoil ended with the stock market crashing to its lowest level for nearly a year....

Financial markets have been unsettled since February when the US federal reserve raised interest rates in what it described as a pre–emptive strike against inflation.... etc.etc.

In the immortal words of Lewis Carroll:

"Will you, won't you, will you, won't you, will you join the dance? (Lewis Carroll)"

Having exported all its investment capital, Britain goes

round with the begging bowl for foreign investment [remember Michael Heseltine, President of the Board of Trade, virtually handing America all the closely guarded secrets of British hi-tech expertise in return for *promises* of participation in the most ludicrous manifestation of production for production's sake ever contemplated – the 'Star Wars' project (see above) – promises never kept; this is known as the special relationship between Britain and the United States] – the only inducement that can be offered: cheap labour power with work more and more difficult to find as computerisation renders more and more skills obsolete.

According to a report in the London Evening Standard (31/1/1994):

> "The Rover Car Company was being sold today to Germany's BMW for £800,000,000 [a nice little earner including a £500,000 'golden handshake' for the M.D. S.T.] less than six years after it was bought by British Aerospace for £150,000,000 [including the famous sweetener' so skilfully negotiated away by Lord Young – another gift from the privateers to the privateers.... S.T.]....*Skyhigh labour costs have been partly (?) responsible for forcing Germany's car makers to look at production opportunities in a relatively low cost economy such as Britain. German Workers are paid an average of £16.90 per hour while their British counterparts receive £8.60.*"[20] [my emphasis S.T.]

---

20. The Rover Car company, despite the large interest of Honda, was the last car manufacturer in British hands. When I was engaged on architectural work for the Ford Motor Company (1950's), it was repeatedly quoted as an axiom that the state of the motor industry was the surest indicator of the state of the economy.

Despite the shortsightedness and inevitable failure of the short term nature of the whole approach as demonstrated above, a huge pool of labour power is created, the extent of which is a closely guarded secret. Figures are massaged (the way in which the numbers of unemployed are counted has been changed some 29 times, each change reducing the figure) and huge numbers of people are do not appear on any list who are employed part time.

The mechanism is simple. Privatise a service, sack all the workers, and then offer *some of them* their jobs back part time at half the rate of pay with a vastly increased work load – they do not appear on any unemployment statistics.

Statistics:

"There are lies, damned lies, and statistics." Mark Twain

Examples.

1) I recently passed a Local Authority building site which was surrounded by a corrugated iron fence. There were about 14 middle aged men in white overalls painting the fence in brown, white, and green diagonal and diamond patterns [production for production's sake – this complicated patterning on a temporary fence

---

served no useful purpose whatsoever that an ordinary coat of paint would not have done – and it was excruciatingly ugly to boot!]. I asked one of the workmen involved what was going on. He replied:

"I used to be a welder, mate. I haven't had a job for four years. I'm what you call your long term unemployed. I'm on a government scheme for a fortnight learning to be a painter [the idea that one can learn to be a painter in two weeks is, of course, ludicrous]."

"Is there a job waiting for you when you finish?" I asked.

"Of course not, mate," he said, "its all a load of crap, but we won't be long term unemployed any more!"

2) According to a letter to The Times (30/12/1993):

"Many commentators are puzzled why official unemployment totals continue to fall when employers are still shedding staff. Not so men and women members of the Over–Fifties Association, and others over 40 who have been made redundant or 'encouraged' into taking early retirement.

"Being fit enough and eager to rejoin the work–force, they sign on and receive unemployment benefit. After 12 months and still unemployed, they no longer receive this benefit, but may then apply for income support.

"However, eligibility for income support rests, among other requirements, on a partner working fewer than 16 hours a week and joint savings not exceeding £3,000 [.0000002% of Mr Peter Wood's average weekly earnings as noted. S.T.]. Even so, many of those made redundant or encouraged into early retirement receive redundancy payments or pension lump sums which, added to their savings, exceed both criteria.

"Because of age discrimination in employment many, though not intending to start a business or incapable of doing so, join the Enterprise Allowance Scheme to secure the allowance, while others are obliged to draw their much reduced occupational pension before normal retirement age. Either action removes them from the unemployment register.

"Three puzzling statistics now become clear: why the average retirement age is 57 and falling rapidly: why new business start-ups are on the increase [a phenomenon hailed by official apologists as hugely optimistic and eulogised as a 'green shoot of recovery'. S.T.]: and why official unemployment figures are falling despite daily reports of companies shedding ever more employees." (Eric Bellenie (Chairman), The Over-Fifties Association.)

3) According to the Guardian (3/1/1994)

"The Government was last night engaged in fresh controversies over claims that child poverty and unemployment levels are far worse than official statistics indicate.

"While the Employment Department denied the findings

of a survey [to quote a classic phrase – "They would, wouldn't they?"] which suggested that true levels of unemployment are between one and two million higher than the official 2.8 million, John Major denounced as "bogus" [which, of course, proves beyond any shadow of doubt that they are! S.T.] claims – backed by Labour MP Frank Field – that the number of children living in poverty had trebled to nearly 3 million since Margaret Thatcher won power in 1979.....

"Employment ministers and officials rejected an analysis [you bet: S.T.] by the Cambridge economist, John Wells, based on International Labour Organisation figures which highlighted the number of people without work who are unable to claim benefit – some 1.08 million [official figures only count people out of work who *are* claiming benefit: S.T.]

"Dr. Wells also includes 306,000 people on government training (?) programmes, which officials reject [you bet: S.T.].

"All measures of unemployment show that it is falling," one said last night [you bet! see examples 1 & 2 above. S.T.].....

"It has long been alleged that 29 changes in jobless definitions [described in the House of Commons by one Tory MP as 'the striving for greater accuracy!' S.T.] may have reduced the total figure by 1 million.[21]

"The row over child poverty is also a recurring one and stems from the huge rise in families living on income support – 1.5 million families, including 2,970,000 children, in 1993, compared with 923,000 children dependent on the old supplementary benefit in 1979, and 272,320 on the original form of poverty support, national assistance, in 1978.

"...[Once again, so much for Mrs. Thatcher's much vaunted 'trickle down' effect, but] ministers have been reluctant to concede that the poor have done badly in the 1980s [you bet¦ S.T.]" (Guardian 3/1/1994).

4) Such proceeds as the government reaps out of privatisation after the dispensing of largesse to its friends are entered into the books as *a reduction in public expenditure.* Proceeds from the sale of NHS assets are, *in complete contradiction* entered into the books as *money put into the National Health Service.* This helps to justify the spurious claim that the government has increased spending on the NHS in real terms. (TV Documentary Programme)

---

21. In a recent play called "Cheek" by Howard Barker, one of the characters said: "It is not our job to cure the disease; our job is to give it a new name. This is the function of modern scholarship." According to the scholarship of official government nomenclature in the person of Peter Lillie, there are no longer any unemployed – there are only 'job–seekers'.

Wealth Creation:

cf: Michael Portillo (Chief Secretary to the Treasury – op. cit.) justifying cuts in the Welfare State: "I really believe that if it [the state] gets any bigger, it is going to place such a burden(!) on the *wealth creating*(!) [my emphasis S.T.] sector of this country that it is going to crush it." (Guardian 25/10/1993 – op cit.)

i.e. wealth–creation = making money.[22]

There is no more insidious piece of obfuscation than the identification of wealth and money, so assiduously disseminated by propagandists and apologists for the system that it would appear to be the most obvious and unproblematic proposition in the world; but, as Brecht once remarked: "When something seems 'the most obvious thing in the world' it means that any attempt to understand the world has been given up!"

What is involved has been searchingly investigated by Andrew Maxwell in a commentary on the writings of Ruskin, (whose errantries on other directions need not concern us here) and the passage which follows is quoted from an article entitled 'On the Notion of "Wealth"', published in the magazine 'Contemporary Issues', Vol 14, No.55. This excellent essay is buried in this virtually forgotten magazine of the 60's and is too

---

22. See remarks on 'enterprise culture' above.

little known. I feel that no apology or justification is required for this extensive quotation, or, rather, the content is its own justification. We have a great heritage of dissent, and I believe every opportunity should be taken to nurture it by reinstatement and quotation. This would especially apply to Heine and Cobbett, whose humourous and, with the exercise of a little imagination, very topical and relevant pieces I have included as an addendum.

"That wealth in commodity society has in the first instance to take the form of money is one of the many things that seem the most obvious thing in the world....[but] the essential point here is to grasp that so little is money or abstract wealth the content of wealth itself that (as Ruskin wrote) "if all the money in the world, notes and gold, were destroyed in an instant, it would leave the world neither richer nor poorer than it was. *But it would leave the individual inhabitants of it in different relations* ('Munera Pulvis' − [my emphasis S.T.]).......

"To start with, what Ruskin wrote about wealth "in itself" may provoke much−needed astonishment:

"It is impossible to conclude [he asserts in 'Unto This Last'] of any given mass of acquired wealth, merely by the fact of its existence, whether it signifies good or evil in the midst of which it exists.....Any given accumulation of commercial wealth may be indicative, on the one hand, of faithful industries, progressive energies, and productive ingenuities; or, on the other, it may be indicative of mortal luxury, merciless tyranny, ruinous chicane...

"One mass of money is the outcome of action which has created – another...of the false direction given to labour, and lying image of prosperity set up...That which seems wealth may in verity be only the index of far–reaching ruin....

"And therefore, the idea that directions can be given for the gaining of wealth, irrespectively of the considerations of its moral sources, or that any general and technical law of purchase and gain can be set down for national practise, is perhaps the most insolently futile of all that ever beguiled men through their vices.

So far as I know, *there is not in history anything so disgraceful to the human intellect as the modern idea that the commercial text "Buy in the cheapest market and sell in the dearest", represents, or under any circumstances, could represent an available principle of national economy.* [my emphasis – tell that to the monetarists! S.T.[23]] ..... One thing only can you know,

---

23. Ruskin had evidently never heard of 'monetarism'. Really, Mr. Ruskin, do you not know that *everything*, including such items as education and public service broadcasting, must be cost effective –i.e. bought cheap and sold dear – or what are *market forces* (the great Gods whom we all worship) all about? According to a report in The Observer (9/1/1994):

"BBC school radio, used by more than 90% of primary schools, is at the centre of a tug of war within the BBC between the corporations traditional commitment to education and the enterprise culture(!) which finds schools broadcasts an expensive encumbrance. *Education appears to be losing the struggle* [my emphasis. S.T.]."

namely, whether this dealing of yours is a just and faithful one, which is all you need concern yourself about respecting it; sure thus to have done your own part in bringing about ultimately in the world a state of things which will not issue in pillage or death."

That the oxygen of the material commodity community is 'pillage and death' forces itself on consciousness at every turn. Indonesia and East Timor; Israel and the Palestinians; The Serbs and Bosnia, Iraq and the Kurds (ably assisted by the West), Central and South America, Somalia, Panama, The Gulf War, The Falklands, Ireland, Cambodia, Angola, Mozambique, **Vietnam** – the list is endless but, finally, as the standing monument to modern barbarism, we have Bosnia, now a bombed out wreck, its beauty smashed, its women systematically raped, its inhabitants starved and gangrenous and Sarajevo – one of the most beautiful cities in the world, a unique centre of cultural cross–fertilisation nestling in spectacular mountain scenery, rased to the ground, its great and irreplaceable libraries burnt to a cinder, its spectacular architectural heritage lost forever, and all happening with the rest of Europe and America calmly looking on.

Despite surface frenetic activity (so–called 'humanitarian' aid and dramatic gestures for the television screens such as flying a few sick children to safety) doomed to built–in failure from the outset, the non-

---

As stated above – it's all a matter of priorities.

intervention militarily amounts to no less than positive connivance and encouragement. Especially relevant must be the embargo on the supply of arms to the Muslims in Bosnia, (an exact parallel to the failure to supply arms to the Hungarians in 1957 despite all the ideological bullshit about 'the defence of democracy') considered in conjunction with the official line on the Muslim 'threat to world peace' – see pages 25 *et seq* above.

With the break–up of the USSR, (the traditional policeman of Eastern Europe, the decentralisation of the Balkans, the 'powder keg of Europe', and the aspiration of small independent states demanding selfdetermination again emerges as a destabilising threat to the world hegemony of America and the West, to gang-sterism itself. Police once again required to swing into action, and who better than Tito's army 'under new management', and all this not 1000 kilometres away from mountains of 'unsaleable' food surpluses and plentiful medical supplies in the midst of a world of abundance which could quite easily have been made available without all the spectacle strictly for the television screens of the 'humanitarian aid' debacle had there been the will to do so. I am not espousing here the 'conspiracy' theory, that these things are all worked out by all parties conspiring together, but that they reflect the inner workings of a system far beyond the control of its human instruments.

Andrew Maxwell continues:

"No need to stress that the wealth of modern society falls completely into the category of gilded index of far-reaching ruin, and that it indicative of mortal luxury , merciless tyranny, ruinous chicane. Inessential errors left aside, what is to be stressed in Ruskin's treatment of wealth is its con-creteness, its attention to its effects in use which determine its character and makes of wealth in general, or *abstract wealth* [my emphasis: S.T.] a meaningless concept."

[It is of course, in the inexorable logic of the system that the pursuit of *abstract wealth* should find its *ultima ratio* in *abstract production,* the production of the means of destruction as the indispensable axle around which the world revolves[24]! S.T.]

"It lies in the nature of his approach of individual respon-

---

24. cf. Stephen Spender (Selected Poems – Faber & Faber MCMXL)

ULTIMA RATIO REGUM

The guns spell money's ultimate reason
In letters of lead on the spring hillside.
But the boy lying dead under the olive trees
Was too young and too silly
To have been notable to their important eye.
He was a better target for a kiss......

Consider his life which was valueless
In terms of employment, hotel ledgers, news files.
Consider. One bullet in ten thousand kills a man.
Ask. Was so much expenditure justified
On the death of one so young and so silly
Lying under the olive trees, O world, O death?

71

sibility in the determination and use of wealth....With this he strikes at the most signal evil of commodity society, the split between theory and social practice [manifesting itself in the ideological sphere as *mendacity! -* see under 'confidentiality' above. S.T.], between principle and performance, essential to it, permitting the constant commission of evil deeds under the mask of good intentions. There is, of course, a sense in which one can, very broadly, admit that the mechanism of commodity society, in particular, competition, compels everyone to behave in appropriately immoral fashion in order to survive; but there is a vast difference (suppressed by interested parties who deal in such fictions as "human nature" to excuse the crimes of the *beati possidentes* of commodity society) between the generality of those who are defenceless victims of the mechanism, and the possessing, ruling minority who consciously delude and cheat the mass of mankind for the sake of profit. They are the unjust and faithless ones Ruskin by implication attacks, whose activities create a state of things which issues in pillage and death, and work for its continuance, and who, therefore, must be accounted responsible for their deeds and their effects. From this point of view, to assert that modern industry, the most striking advances of which are virtually restricted to means of destruction in all spheres [or to 'spin-offs' from same' S.T.] is one gigantic cheat, is to assert the unfortunately too unobvious obvious. Considered from the aspect of its end, exchange for profit, it is described with telling accuracy by Ruskin as follows:

"The Science of Exchange, or, as I hear it has been proposed to call it, of "Catallectics"...considered as one of acquisition, is a very curious science, differing in its

72

data and basis from every other science known: thus:–
If I can exchange a needle with a savage for a diamond,
my power of doing so depends either on the savage's
ignorance of social arrangements in Europe, or on his
want of power to take advantage of them by selling the
diamond to anyone else for more needles. If, further, I
make the bargain as completely advantageous to myself
as possible, by giving the savage a needle with no eye
in it (reaching, thus, a sufficiently satisfactory type of
the catallectic science), the advantage to me in the entire
transaction depends wholly upon the ignorance, *power –
lessness* [my emphasis – compare price–fixing by mo-
nopolies and cartels, transnational corporations, etc.
S.T.] or heedlessness of the person dealt with.[25] Do
away with these, and catallectic advantage becomes
impossible....."

"That the very foundation of commodity society, the pos-
sibility of its constant self–increasing abstract wealth in the
form of capital, lies in this "perfect operation of catallectic
science" and the enforced maintenance of powerlessness of
the opposite persons required by it, in buying something for
nothing and selling nothing for something (surplus value,
the purest example of which is Russian slave labour at the
time of Stalin) is in its phenomenal form of wage labour,
with its effects upon the person of the labourer, his health
and happiness, clear to Ruskin. For all that he does not
grasp the matter fully in its essential import, he perceives,

---

25. "In bourgeois society the "legal fiction" prevails that every
person, as buyer of commodities, has an encyclopedic knowledge
of them" K.Marx, Capital, Chapter 1. This is enshrined in the law
which states "caveat emptor!" – Let the purchaser beware!

and this is the crucial point, that this fraud runs through the whole of commodity society, and is the specific character of its production and exchange, namely, of the creation[!] of its particular kind of [abstract] wealth....With "built-in obsolescence" as a deliberate artifice to support the production of masses of useless and mostly harmful trash [and *abstract production* as the apotheosis of production itself: S.T.] it reaches the zenith of 'insolent fraud and faithlessness' beyond anything Ruskin could have imagined. The whole becomes (in the words of Gabor) "a system which can run only by keeping a maelstrom of paper and goods milling round towards a gigantic drain". More accurately, it is the very life-blood of man and nature recklessly transformed into a maelstrom of waste, that is poured away into this gigantic drain, impoverishing the world and poisoning the very springs of life along the whole of its course....

"It is plain that abstract commodity wealth [for the 'creating' sector of which creatures like Michael Portillo exhibit such concern. S.T.] as a thing and end in itself is, by reason of this very fact, necessarily left to its own lawless flow and has become...the last and deadliest of universal plagues which feeds the roots of all evil and is incapable of doing anything else."

Notwithstanding the blather about 'wealth creation', it is clear: the first and last incentive of the capitalist mode of production, the be-all and end-all, is *profit,* which realises itself through buying cheap and selling dear, and is accumulated in order to survive in the competitive struggle. The whole system centres around the needs of capital, which has the effect of a self-reliant impersonal power independent of the human will, and the needs of capital are the axis around which the single individuals centre. Slaves of the system are we all – in this sense capitalism is tragic, and can never be reformed, but only *eliminated.*

This, at least, must be the *most obvious thing in the world!*

ADDENDUM

SOME REFLECTIONS

1) Heinrich Heine

"Last summer I came to know a philosopher in Bedlam, who with stealthy eyes and whispering voice gave me many important disclosures about the origin of evil. Like many of his colleagues he also thought that in this matter you must accept something historical. Concerning myself, I readily agreed to such an acceptance, and declared that the root of the evil in the world was due to the circumstance that the good God has created too little money.

""It is very easy for you to talk," answered the philosopher, "the good God was very hard up at Kassa when He created the world. For that purpose, He was obliged to borrow money from the devil, and to make over to him the whole creation as hypothec. As a consequence, the good God in due legal form still owes the world to him, so also He may, out of delicacy, not prevent him from disporting himself therein, and causing confusion and mischief. But the devil for his part has again a very strong personal interest that the world should not utterly perish, as thereby the hypothec should be lost. He takes care, therefore, to make it as stupid as possible, and the good God, who for his part is not stupid, knows well that He has His secret guarantee in the self–interest of the devil.

""Thus He goes so far as to intrust the whole government of the world to him, that is to say, He gives the devil instructions to form a Ministry. Then it happens as a matter of course that Samiell obtains command of the hellish hosts, Beelzebub becomes Chancellor, Vitziputzli becomes Secretary of State, the old grandmother gets the Colonies, and so on.

""These confederates then administer affairs after their own fashion, and whilst they, notwithstanding the evil of their own hearts, themselves constrained out of self interest to further the welfare of the world, they yet indemnify themselves somewhat in that they always make use of the basest means for good purposes. Of late, indeed, they carried matters so badly that even Gods in his heaven could no longer behold such enormity, and accordingly gave an angel instructions to form the new Ministry.

""This angel gathered around him all good spirits. Joyful enthusiasm pervaded the world again; it became light, and the evil spirits vanished. Still they did not quietly fold their claws in their laps; they worked secretly against everything good, they poisoned the new sources of prosperity, they spitefully crushed every blossom of the new spring. With their amendments they destroyed the tree of life, chaotic destruction threatened to engulf everything, so that in the end the good God will again have to transfer the government to the devil in order that the evil spirits, through their worst efforts, may derive the least benefit.

""Thus thou seest the evil effects of a debt."

"This communication of my friend in Bedlam explains perhaps the present change in the English Ministry....It cannot be denied that after Canning's death the Whigs were not in a position to maintain the peace of England, because the measures they had on that account to take were being continually being defeated by the Tories.

"The King, to whom the preservation of the public peace, that is, the security of his throne, appears the most important matter, must perforce again give over the administration of the state to the Tories. And oh! they will now again as before administer all the fruits of the industry of the people into their own treasury. Like Jewish speculators, they will run up the price of grain, until John Bull, becoming meagre with hunger, will at last for a morsel of bread sell himself to those high masters who will put him at the plough, and beat him till he dare not once even grumble. Then on the one side the Duke of Wellington will threaten him with the sword, and on the other side the Archbishop of Canterbury will knock him on the head with the bible – and there will be peace in the land.

"The source of this evil is the National Debt, or, as Cobbett call it, the King's Debt. Cobbett quite rightly remarks, for example, that while one places in the front of all institutions the name of the King, as 'the King's army', 'the King's navy',

'the King's courts', 'the King's prison's'. etc., yet, notwith-
standing, the great debt which really owes it origins to those
institutions is never called the King's debt; and it is the only
institution by which the nation is shown the honour of
having something named after her.

"The worst of the evil is the debt. True enough, it enables
the English state to preserve itself, so that even its basest
devil cannot destroy it; but at the same time it is also the
reason why the whole of England is become a large tread-
mill, where the people must work day and night to pay its
creditors.

"Hence it also arises that England becomes weaned from all
youthful joyful yearnings, and bends a grey head over the
cares of accounting."

Note: The perspicacity of Heine's insight has an
immediate impact.

The characteristic most remarked by all visitors to
England from abroad is the air of deep depression and
hopelessness which hangs like a pall over the whole
country – the homeless sleeping under doorways or in
'cardboard cities' in London and confronting theatre-
goers; the decayed inner city centres; the prevalence of
'alkis' or 'wine–os': the fear of walking alone in the
streets: open drug–gang warfare etc.; de–industrialised;
de–infra–structured; the destruction of educational,
health, and social support services now far advanced.

Even the 'circuses' asserted by Bismarck to be so

essential for maintaining the morale of the masses in their misery so that the government can get on with the job without interference collapse coincidentally – the inability to start a horse race (high jinks at the Grand National); ignominious defeat on the football field and failure to qualify for the World Cup (accompanied by the breakdown of social mores in the form of hooliganism, both spontaneous ("the riot is the festival of the oppressed" – how else to express frustration?) and fomented (by fascists – after all, are not frustration and deprivation the breeding ground for fascism?); other sporting arenas (cricket, tennis etc, where the establishment can do no more than provide the setting); the inability to provide a decent piano for the Leeds International Piano Competition – all the competitors complained that the mechanism of the piano was too hard to produce a proper *pianissimo* (the organisers had in fact been warned about this by the piano tuner, but the warning had been ignored – after all, he was only a common working man; what did *he* know?) as well as the decision to cut funding to two of London's four major symphony orchestras.

"Why should we give money to the Arts anyway?" asked one MP, "We should devote it to doing something useful!" [26] The cuts threatening the Arts amount to a miserable £5,000,000 (to judge just how miserable cf: "Constituents of the Debt" above). I would have

---

26. cf: Herman Goerring: "When I hear the word culture, I reach for my revolver!.

thought that the Chairman of the Arts Council, multi-millionaire property developer and alleged lover of the arts, Mr Peter (now Lord) Palumbo could have given it to them out of petty cash – instead he masterminded the whole affair.

In the event, the public outcry forced them to return to the *status quo ante,* but no wonder this government, or this administration, or this establishment, or these rulers, or, if you will, this government was described by the Wall Street Journal as "behind their plush velvet seats and their armed guards, strutting like peacocks on top of a rotting museum."

Heine continues:

"Thus it generally happens with all men heavily in debt, they are ground down in dull resignation, and do not know how to help themselves – although 900,000 guns and just as many swords and bayonets lie stored in the Tower of London, yet the well–fed red–coated beefeaters who are on guard there could be easily over–powered......

"Debts, just as patriotism, religion and honour, belong, it is true to the privileges of men – the lower animals being exempt; but debts are also quite the pre–eminent affliction of mankind, and as they ruin individuals, so they also bring nations to ruin. The appear to restore the old Fate in the national tragedies of our time. England cannot escape this Fate: its Ministers sees it horrors approaching, and die with the despair of impotence.

Were I Royal Prussian Lands–Evaluator, or a civil engineer, I should calculate in the usual way, and reduce the whole sum of the English debt into *silber groschen,* and then accurately tell how many times I should cover these with the *Grosse Friedrichstrasse,* or even the whole earth ball. But calculating was never my forte, and I should prefer giving up to an Englishman the fatal business of counting his debts and thence reckoning the actual necessities of the Ministry. For this work there is no man more competent than old [or should we say 'the great'? S.T.] Cobbett, and I give the following arguments from the last number of his *Political Register.*[27]

2) William Cobbett

1) This Government – or on the contrary, this aristocracy and Church, or, if you will, this Government – borrowed a large sum of money with which she has purchased many victories[28] by land and sea, a number of victories of every sort and size.

---

27. Writing under the Peter Porcupine, Cobbett's Weekly Political Register became famous, appearing from 1802 until 1835. In 1837, the Chartists were already on the march with Cobbett's demands (universal suffrage etc).

28. See 'Constituents of the Debt' above. Unfortunately the 'purchases' of this government, or, on the contrary, this aristocracy and Church, or this administration, or this establishment, or these rulers, or, if you will, this government, are by no means confined to such occasions for celebration as 'victories'.

2) Meanwhile, I must premise by inquiring why and wherefore these victories were bought. The occasion was the French Revolution, which had made an end of *aristocratic privileges* and *clerical tithes*; and the purpose was the prevention of a Parliamentary Reform in England, which would most likely resulted in a similar destruction of all aristocratic privileges and clerical tithes.

3) Now in order to prevent the example of the French from being imitated by the English, it was necessary to lay hold on the French, to arrest their progress, to endanger their newly acquired freedom, to force them to desperate acts , and at last to make the Revolution such a source of terror and dismay to the people that, under the name of freedom, they pictured to themselves nothing but an aggregate of wickedness, horror, and bloodshed. Thus the English people themselves would become, through the inspiration of fear, even actually enamoured with that horrible despotic government that once blossomed in France, notwithstanding that every Englishman detested it from the days of Alfred the Great to those of the Georges.

4) In order to bring about those designs the co-operation of various nations was needful. Those nations were actually subsidised with English money – French immigrants were maintained with English money – in short, a twenty-two years war was carried on in order to crush that people who had risen against *aristocratic privileges* and *clerical tithes.*

5) Our Government further gained *'numberless victories'* over the French who, as it appears, were always beaten. But these our 'numberless victories' were bought, that is. they were achieved by mercenary troops hired with our money;

and we had in our pay, at one and the same time, whole squadrons of French, Dutch, Swiss, Italian, Russian, Austrian, Bavarian, Hessian, Hanoverian, Prussian, Spanish, Portuguese, Neapolitan, Maltese, and God knows how many nations besides.[29]

6) By such hiring of foreign services and by the use of our own fleet and land forces, we *bought* so many victories over the French – who, poor devils! had no money to enable them to purchase them in the same manner – that we at last overwhelmed their Revolution, and restored the aristocracy in a certain degree, although we could not by any means restore the clerical tithes in equal degree.

7) After we had satisfactorily perfected this great work, and had also counteracted Parliamentary Reform in England, our government raised a lusty cry of victory, whereby she strained her lungs not a little, and in this effort of shouting was loudly supported by every creature in the land who benefitted by public taxation.

8) For nearly two years this successful nation revelled in the

---

29. Compare the antics of the Americans just before the Gulf War rushing round to all the Middle East nations (Saudi Arabia etc.) with huge bribes to give the affair the semblance of an international force. So as not wreck the charade, Israel, America's traditional policeman in the Middle East, was also warned not to intervene (even when under attack from missiles) and was included in the bribery, but the British, of course, didn't need any bribing – they just dutifully wagged their tails like faithful doggies and barked after their masters (getting shot up by them into the bargain) and cheerfully allowed British soldiers to be bombed and bombarded with armaments supplied to the 'enemy' by Britain.

intoxication of exuberant joy. In order to celebrate those victories there swarmed everywhere jubilations, public games, triumphal arches, military reviews, and the like amusements at cost of more than a quarter of a million sterling. I believe that the House of Commons voted unanimously the enormous sum of three millions sterling in order to erect triumphal arches, monumental columns, and statuary by which to immortalise *the glorious event of war.*

9) Ever since that time we have had the good fortune to live under the Government of the same personages who had conducted our affairs during this glorious war.

10) Ever since that time we have lived at profound peace with all the world; and this is still the case notwithstanding our little skirmishes with the Turks [or the Irish, or the Argentinians, or the Iraqi etc. S.T.]. Consequently there would seem to be no reason in the world why we should not be happy now. We have peace, to be sure, our land yields its fruit in abundance, and as the philosophers and lawgivers of our time admit, we are the most enlightened nation on the whole earth. We have [had? S.T.] schools, to be sure, everywhere in order to instruct the rising generation; not only have we a rector or vicar or curate in every diocese of the kingdom, but we have besides in every diocese perhaps six other teachers of religion – each differing from the other – so that our land is sufficiently provided with instructions of every sort, and no man of this fortunate land may live in a state of ignorance. Therefore our amazement must be so much greater when we find a Prime Minister of this fortunate land regarding his duties as so heavy and grievous a burden.

11) Ah! we have a single misfortune, and this is a great one; we have bought some victories – they were glorious – it was a good piece of business – they were three or four times better than we paid for, as Mrs. Tweazle said to her husband when she came home from the market. There was a great enquiry and demand for victories; in short, we could not do better than provide ourselves so cheaply with such a large amount of glory.

12) But I confess it with sorrow, we have, like many other people, *borrowed* the money to buy these *victories* of which we now can in no way get rid, any more than a man can get rid of his wife once he has had the good fortune to take such a fair burden upon his shoulders.

13) Thus it happens that every Minister who undertakes our affairs must also provide for the payment of our victories, whereof no penny has yet been paid.

14) It is true he does not need to provide for the payment of capital and interest all at once; but he must, in God's pity, most certainly provide for the *interest,* the pay of the army, and other expenses arising out of our *victories.* He must therefore be a man of pretty strong nerves if he undertakes this little business.

15) Before we meddled with buying victories to satiate ourselves with glory, we already bore a debt of little more than *two hundred millions,* whilst all the parochial relief in England and Wales did not amount to more than *two millions* per annum. Then we had nothing of that burden which is now laid upon us under the name of *Dead Weight,* and which has arisen entirely from our thirst for glory.

16) Besides this *borrowed money* our government has also *indirectly* [my emphasis – S.T.] raised a great loan from the *poor*, by increasing the common taxes [see p.27 *et. seq.* S.T.] to such a height that the poor were ground down far more than formerly, in consequence the number of paupers and the amount of parochial relief were simultaneously decreased to an astonishing degree.

17) The poor–rates rose from *two millions* to *eight millions* yearly: the poor have now, as it were, the right of mortgages, an hypothec on the land. Hence results also the gain of a debt of *six millions in addition to those other debts that our passion for glory and the purchase of our victories* have occasioned.

18) The *Dead Weight* consists of annuities granted in the names of pensions to a multitude of men, women and children in respect of services which those men have, or ought to have rendered towards the achievement of our victories.

19) The capital of the debt which this Government had contracted in order to create victories for itself may be roughly estimated as follows:

Capitalized sum of the National Debt	800,000,000
Capitalised sum of Poor Rates	150,000,000
Dead Weight to be reckoned as a Capital Debt	175,000,000
Total: Sterling	£1,125,000,000

That is to say, *eleven hundred and twenty five millions* sterling, at five per cent. interest per annum, represents an annual payment of fifty–six millions. Indeed this is about the present amount, only that the *Parochial Relief Debt* does not appear in the accounts that are submitted to Parliament, because the land bears its burden directly in the different parishes. If therefore you deduct that six millions or so of the poor rates from the fifty–six millions, it follows that the creditors of the National Debt and the *Dead Weight* people actually swallow up all that is left.

20) But all the same, the poor rates are just as much a *debt* as a debt of the creditors of the National Debt, and obviously spring from the same sources. By the terrible burden of taxation the poor were crushed down. It is true that every other person was also oppressed, but everyone except the poor knew how to throw this burden more or less from his shoulders, and it fell at last with terrible weight wholly on the poor. They lost their beer–barrels, their copper kettles, their pewter plates, their clocks, their beds, and everything even to their tools. They lost their clothes and were obliged to wrap themselves in rags. They lost the flesh from their bones – they could not be driven to more dire extremity – and of that which was taken from them, they received something back under the name of increased parochial relief. This is therefore a *true debt*, a true right of a bond holder on the land. The interest of this debt could, it is true, be withheld, but if this were attempted the persons who should demand it would approach in masses and get themselves paid in full, no matter in what currency. *This is then a **true debt**, and a debt that will have to be paid down on the nail, and I positively assert that it will be allowed the preference over all other debts.*

21) Accordingly it is no great wonder when you see the

trouble of those (Ministers) who undertake such affairs! The chief wonder is that any of them should ever undertake their management, if he were not empowered to bring about as he thought best a radical change of the whole system. [This is, of course, the last thing that those who worship the 'wealth–creating' sectors of society would want – the answer to Cobbett's question is that these ministers are no more than faithful and obedient servants to the masters they serve. S.T.].

22) The two first–named debts, to wit, the National Debt and the *Dead–Weight* debt were formerly paid – or to put it better, interest was formerly paid – in a depreciated paper money of whose value fifteen shillings were scarcely worth a Winchester bushel of wheat. This was the manner in which the national creditors were paid for many years. But in the year 1819, a profound statesman, Mr. Peel, made the great discovery that it was better for the nation to pay their debts in hard cash, of which five shillings instead of fifteen shillings in paper money were worth as much as a Winchester bushel of wheat.

23) The *nominal sum* was never changed![30] It always remained the same; nothing happened but that Mr. Peel and the Parliament *had changed its value..* It was their desire that the debt should be paid in the form of coin, of which five shillings, after much reckoning, were found to be of as much value as fifteen shillings of the paper money *wherein the debt was contracted and wherein the interest had been paid during many years.*

---

30. Axiom as quoted above for all times: Currency Manipulation = Swindling of the People!

24) Thence it followed that from 1819 to the present day the nation lived in the most disconsolate condition [!]. It was eaten upon by its creditors, who were mostly Jews, or rather Christians who acted like Jews, and who were not so easily persuaded to rush the less greedily on their prey.

25) Many an attempt was made in order to mitigate in some of the consequences of the change which took place in the value of money in 1819; but these attempts failed, and had once almost sprung the whole thing into the air.

26) There is no possibility of relief in seeking to reduce the annual payments to the creditors of the National Debt and of the *Dead–Weight* Debt. In order to effect so much a reduction of the debt, just so much a reduction must be exacted from the land [read: the people. S.T.] – in order to prevent it from bringing about great revolutions – in order that half a million people, in and about London, may not die of hunger. Therefore it is necessary to undertake before-hand greater proportional reductions *elsewhere* [e.g. in the PSBR by raising taxes. S.T.] *before* attempting the reduction the above two debts or their interest.

27) As we have already seen, the victories were already bought with intention of opposing Parliamentary reform in England, and to maintain aristocratic privileges and clerical tithes. It would therefore be a revolting atrocity did we deprive those people who borrowed the money for us, of their legal interest, or even were we to deprive of payment those people who hired out the hands that procured our victories. It would be a horrible deed, that would draw down upon us the wrath of Heaven if we perpetrated it whilst the honorary places of the aristocracy, their pensions,

"HERE, HERE, THEREFORE, LIES
THE DIFFICULTY"

sinecures, royal grants, military rewards, and lastly, while even the tithes of the clergy remained inviolate.

28) *Here, here,* therefore lies the difficulty. He who will be Minister will be Minister of a land which has had a great passion for *victories* – which has sufficiently provided itself with victories and created unheard-of glories, and now hands over the reckoning to the Minister, who knows not wherewithal he will get the money to pay.

APPENDIX

1. Treasury forecasts come under the rubric of 'The Games Governments Play'. According to the Guardian (28/3/1994):

> "The Financial Times reported that in the run-up to Norman Lamont's pre-election March budget the Treasury had inklings of how rapidly the government's fiscal position was to deteriorate – even if it was 12 months later before it published its famous forecast of a £50 billion PSBR. In its first projections before the budget, it forecast the PSBR in 1993/1994 would be £40 billion – but was told by Mr Lamont in an internal note to "massage" the figures downwards, reported the FT. The projection of £32 billion was duly published."

From £32 billion to £50 billion in 12 months – only £18 billion adrift. Would you buy a second-hand car from *him*? It would in fact be an easily sustainable position to say that never in the history of human endeavour has a Treasury forecast proved to be correct.

2. Britain thrown out of the Exchange Rate Mechanism, notwithstanding categorical assertions by both Norman Lamont and John Major that member-ship of the ERM was the corner-stone of British economic policy – figure quoted on British Television Documentary programme. When tackled on the subject in a recent BBC programme (Question Time), Mr. Portillo [Secretary to the Treasury and personally responsible for the Poll Tax fiasco (see note 3 below)], could come up with no other reply but that the policy of membership of the ERM had the backing of the Labour Party, as though that made it all right! Response from the Labour Party representative on the panel – a deafening silence.

3. BBC television documentary op. cit. – this includes administration costs, computerisation (having had to be completely redone several times as the rules were changed), fees, additional staff, etc. The programme stated that this money, the whole £3,500,000,000, might just as well have been put on a bonfire in Hyde Park and set alight. This, however, did not deter the police from mounting a military operation against demonstrators exercising their right to protest and then bring them to court, all in line with the government's deliberate policy of criminalising demonstrations. This is now being enshrined in law in the new so–called Criminal Justice Bill.

4. Figure from CND, confirmed by Greenpeace – covers all costs including decommissioning.

5. According to a report in The Guardian (25/10/1993):

"Up to £100,000,000 has been spent by the Ministry of Defence to rectify serious problems with a *top secret* [my emphasis. S.T.] bunker built under Whitehall for the Prime Minister and military chiefs....The Treasury has already had to accept a £500,000,000 bill to re–equip MI5 and MI6 in their new headquarters...In 1990 and 1991 huge sums were allocated to the secret project to the anger of the Treasury...The row broke out when the Treasury discovered [when thieves fall out...S.T.] that the MoD (Ministry of Defence) wanted millions of pounds more to rectify mistakes because the bunker could not be used properly.... [!?. – see Glossary: 'abstract production'. S.T.] The MoD also admits that it has, in effect, misled Parliament by, in its words, 'scattering the costs across various headings in the Appropriation Accounts...The only clues the Guardian could find to the overspend are two entries under the Defence Works Services budget in 1990/91 & 1991/92. The 1990/91 account records a £16,800,000 over spend on £804,000,000 of unnamed capital projects while the 1991/92 accounts records a £13,360,000 overspend under the heading 'underestimation of expenditure on property management' *The property manage-ment budget for that year is marked as more than £1 billion"*

Under the circumstances the estimation of £1,500,000,000 in the table would appear really quite modest.

6. According to the Guardian (3/1/1994)

"Allan Milburn, [MP for Darlington and] chairman of Labour's back bench Treasury committee, last night produced new data, culled from Treasury parliamentary answers, that revealed the scale of upper rate tax cuts since 1988...."The Tories are acting like Robin Hood in reverse – stealing from the many to pay for the privileges of the few.....These figures show that in the four years after Nigel Lawson's 1988 Budget cut top rate taxes, £13.8 billion has gone into the pockets of the wealthiest people in Britain."

A gift from the privateers of Britain to the privateers of Britain indeed! See Glossary: 'Privatisation'.

7. Ministry of Defence: Costs & Receipts Arising from the Gulf Conflict. Report by Controller & Auditor General, National Audit Office, printed by Order of the House of Commons.

8. Supply Estimates, 1993–1994. HMSO

9. Documents consulted:

HMSO: Cm 2230: Supply Estimates, Summary & Guide, 1993.
HMSO: Appropriation Accounts, 1992 – 1993, Vol.11:XI
HMSO: Supply Estimates Class 1 M. o. D., March 1993

No figure could be gleaned from these documents, study of which made it hard to believe there really is a military presence in Northern Ireland. The figure quoted was given to me by Ken Livingstone, MP, with permission to quote him as my authority.